# NETWORK POWER

The Science of Making a Difference

David John Seel, Jr.

WHITHORN PRESS

St. Andrew's Academy
Chester/Lake Almanor, California

Published 2021 by
Whithorn Press, St. Andrew's Academy
P.O. Box 3050 Chester, CA 96020

978-1-7373318-1-0

*Dedicated to*
*Kathryn Powell Seel*
*Real Friend, Real Partner, Real Love*

# PRAISE FOR NETWORK POWER

"While the vast majority of leaders in America are obsessed with inspirational quotes and how they can "make an impact," John Seel has focused on what really changes the world. His new book, *Network Power* is the handbook for how to actually influence this culture. If you're serious about making a difference, then it's time to understand the power of organizations uniting in a compelling cause. In today's digital age, this is the path forward."
— Phil Cooke, Ph.D.
  Filmmaker and media consultant,
  and author of *Maximize Your Influence*


"In an era of self-proclaimed 'change makers,' we have lost sight of how change actually happens. In *Network Power*, my friend John Seel draws on theory, history and a lifetime of experience to make a case about how real, lasting and meaningful change happens in a society. Leaders can draw on the lessons of this book to act with purpose, even in chaotic times.".
— Michael Wear
  Founder of Public Square Strategies, LLC., and author of *Reclaiming Hope: Lessons Learned in the Obama White House About the Future of Faith in America*

"*Network Power* goes against the grain of what many leaders assume to be true of cultural change. Seel relies on studies of "network science" in recent years in order to advocate for the "dense network" (and not the genius or celebrity) as most vital for engaging the culture. You'll find this work to be provocative in the best sense of the world: —challenging long-held perspectives in light of new studies, with an eye to effecting change in society."
— Trevin Wax
    Author of *Rethink Your Self:*
    *The Power of Looking Up Before Looking In*


"An African proverb states, "'If you want to go fast, *go alone*. If you want to go far, *go together*.'" Dense networks are an incarnation of *going together*. My intellectual interlocutor, John Seel, traces historically the cultural impact and import of dense networks. Methodically, and with great precision, Seel shows us that leveraging these dense networks is not only wise, resourceful, sustainable, but most importantly God-honoring. And because the cultural influence of dense networks transcends time and space (Seel provides examples of contemporary dense networks), this volume will be one you come back to repeatedly."
— Luke Bobo
    Director of Strategic Partnerships at Made to Flourish


"John Seel brings an interdisciplinary approach that showcases why some organizations have succeeded in their fields. This framework, based in community and relationship, can heighten the effectiveness of any group, large or small. The principles of dense networks are simple but not simplistic and I would recommend keeping this book on your shelf as you will want to return to these ideas regularly."
— Matt Burke
    Director, Center on Congregations

# CONTENTS

# INTRODUCTION

# MAKING A DIFFERENCE USING DENSE NETWORKS

*"Give me a lever long enough and a fulcrum on which to place it, and I shall move the world."*[1]
— Archimedes

This is a book about leveraging your impact. Every person and organization want to make a difference in the world. They can, but not alone.

Many churches, non-profits, and corporations have latent networks of members, employees, customers, alumni, and suppliers. Few of these latent networks are mobilized to be effective in furthering the influence and mission of the parent organization. This is wasted social capital.

We are hardwired for significance. We all want our lives to count. A characteristic of modern life is the feeling that we make no difference. We feel we are nothing more than an anonymous cog in a giant wheel that is unknown and insignificant. Modernity accentuates this feeling of isolation and impotence.

There is a narrative that seeks to counter these feelings; people who want to underscore that your life has a purpose. An entire industry of self-help instruction has been created to further this counter-narrative. While there is truth in this counter-narrative: every person has a calling and this calling has eternal significance for all who believe in a loving, sovereign God. But the stumbling block to this counter-narrative is its emphasis on individualism,

---

[1] Jeanne Bendick. *Archimedes and the Door of Science* (Ignatius Press, 2001), p. 39.

which we will discuss. As we will see, it is not the individual who matters most, but the group, and in this case a particular kind of group, a dense network. Walter Isaacson observes the same reality in his book, *The Innovators*. The key actor in science and technological innovation is not individual genius, but rather the network, and the new institutions that are created out of these networks. The technological revolution is actually a story of collaborative creativity.[2]

The dense network is the main actor on the stage of lasting cultural change, both now and in the past. Dense networks were the main actors in the rise of Christianity, abolition of slavery, the rise of Russian communism, Jewish admission to elite universities, the civil rights movement, and the LGBTQ+ equality movement. They are the way things get done.

A dense network is a formal relationally oriented or ideologically oriented diverse group of friends, colleagues, or acquaintances that share a common commitment to making a difference in the world in a particular arena of social life. They share a common mission or organizational solidarity and overlapping relationships or organizational sociability. It is the dense network that leverages a cause within a particular social world. The laws of a dense network then are just as rooted in reality as the physics of leverage. Using the familiar picture of a lever, we will examine the main parts of a dense network and how it functions to maximize cultural impact. For maximum impact, we will have to create a lever, place it on a fulcrum, and connect it to a specific world.

**Called to Practical Discernment**
Corporate, nonprofit, and faith-based leaders are looking for practical wisdom, to be able to assess the signs of the times, and the way they should go. Network science has much to offer; however, information about the power of networks is academically siloed. The insights we need to be more effective in our callings

---

[2] Walter Issacson. *The Innovators: How a Group of Hackers, Geniuses, and Geeks Created the Digital Revolution* (Simon & Schuster, 2015).

and organizations are often fragmented across the fields of marketing, economics, mathematics, sociology, anthropology, and epidemiology, among others. The effort here is to compile these insights and place them into a simple practical metaphor of a lever and fulcrum capable of moving your world.

At the end of this book is a Resource section that provides a list of definitions of sociological terms used in this book as well as a summary of the social dynamic rules discussed here. The goal here is to accelerate your potential impact in society—to maximize your potential as an organization.

# A RELATIONAL REALITY
## Why Our Previous Approaches Haven't Worked

*"What physicists and contemplatives alike are confirming*
*is that the foundational nature of reality is relational;*
*everything is in a relationship with everything else."*[3]
— Father Richard Rohr, OFM

Any person or organization that is keen on making a difference within a particular arena of society must take the necessity of dense networks seriously. Without engaging dense networks in service to your cause or organizational mission, you will tend to spin your wheels, talk only to yourself, and ultimately make no appreciable long-term social difference. Put bluntly, social engagement without the power of dense networks is not really social engagement.

### Barriers to Influence
American society places a high value on individualism. We tend to place greater value on the heroic individual or the genius innovator than the network of relationships in which they are embedded. People talk about making a difference, but actually very little happens. University of Virginia sociologist James Davison Hunter warns of this in his *To Change the World*, but his warnings largely fell on deaf ears. He states unequivocally, "Every strategy and tactic for changing the world that is based on this working theory of culture [the aggregate of individual effort] and cultural change will fail—not most of these strategies, but all."[4] What we see adopted as strategies of cultural change are usually

---

[3] Richard Rohr, OFM. *The Divine Dance: The Trinity and Your Transformation* (Whitaker House, 2016), p. 69.
[4] James Davison Hunter. *To Change the World* (Oxford University Press, 2010), p. 27.

individual efforts on steroids. Here is a sampling of six wrong approaches.

## Six Ineffective Approaches

First is the assumption that cultural change is the result of getting the right person into a position of leadership. Here, the focus is on the individual and maximizing his or her platform of fame. It is for this reason that we champion the celebrity spokesperson. The problem with this approach is that it is not primarily the individual that matters as much as the group. As we will see in our first case study of more significance in the English fight against abolition was the Clapham Circle as much as William Wilberforce. The lone individual is not the main force in the dynamics of cultural change.

The second wrong approach is to think that cultural change can be achieved through political coercion or mass mobilization. To our preoccupation with the individual, we add power, and, in particular, state power as expressed in politics. This has been the favorite approach of the faith community for the past forty years. The problem is that it exerts influence and orients its strategic focus in the wrong place. In effect, the church has been addressing symptoms, not causes. When one acknowledges that "culture is upstream from politics," one is simply stating that cultural change cannot be achieved through political effort. [5] The rules and dynamics of politics differ from that of culture. We are playing Hearts when the game is Spades. We are often seen to be playing by the wrong rules in the wrong game. To be effective, we need to enter the cultural arena on its own terms and according to its own internal logic. To play the wrong game by the wrong rules is, as Hunter warned, a recipe for failure.

---

[5] The spiritual is upstream from culture or to put it otherwise culture is an expression of what we worship, and thus in many cases an expression of our idolatries. See Steven Garber, "Culture Is Upstream from Politics," https://murdocktrust.org/2020/06/the-culture-is-upstream-from-politics/. Richard John Neuhaus wrote, "Culture is the root of politics, and religion is the root of culture." https://www.firstthings.com/richard-john-neuhaus-society/.

A third wrong approach is to assume that culture operates on the basis of the free market. All that is needed, this approach suggests, is to call people to make cultural products and enter them into the wider dynamics of free market exchange. While all persons are called to make cultural products that reflect the good, true, and beautiful, this is not a comprehensive strategy for cultural change. The dynamics of culture do not follow the dictates of markets—whether we are talking about art pieces or film scripts. Whereas this approach has the benefit of moving people beyond talk to action (actually making things), it is action that assumes individualism. There is action to be taken, but it needs to be aligned with the physics of cultural dynamics, not market forces. The approaches of the celebrity, politician, and businessman will not do.

A fourth wrong approach is to place the emphasis on polemics, in particular the need for adopting a correct worldview or ideological perspective. This approach assumes that if enough people collectively adopt a particular worldview that culture will inevitably change. This approach has the added error of adopting a false anthropology, assuming that if we get our thinking right, we'll get our behavior right and if enough of us do this, culture will change. Philosopher James K.A. Smith laments this common approach. He writes, "Many Christian schools, colleges, and universities—particularly in the Protestant tradition—have taken on board a picture of human persons that owes more to modernity and the Enlightenment [the intellectual movement of the 17th and 18th century] than it does to the holistic, biblical vision of human persons. In particular, Christian education has absorbed a philosophical anthropology that sees human beings as primarily thinking things."[6] When spirituality is reduced to worldview, it is reduced to "a set of ideas, principles, claims, and propositions that are known and believed." Smith concludes, "The operative notion of worldview has been tied to a stunted, rationalist picture of the human person; in short, 'worldview' has gotten hitched to the

---

[6] James K.A. Smith. *Desiring the Kingdom* (BakerAcademic, 2009), p. 31.

wagon of a misguided philosophical anthropology."[7] So this approach has the problem of being wrong both in anthropology as well as sociology. So, to the celebrity, politician, and businessman, we can add the educator and pastor.

A fifth approach focuses on positive psychology, suggesting that if persons are well- adjusted, empowered with self-esteem, or reinforced with gratitude or happiness that culture will change. This too is individualistic in its approach and only serves to change the dynamics to a psychological state. The psychological states being considered here tend to be based on observable behavior. This is a problem in that 95% of our action is shaped by our unconscious dispositions.[8] Almost all of our conscious thought is culturally conditioned, historically derived attitudes and approaches to life. French social theorist Pierre Bourdieu called this "history swallowed."[9] More important to the dynamics of cultural change are the hidden unconscious dispositions, which like so many other aspects of the dynamics of cultural change are generally ignored. Failure is inevitable when this is the case. The therapist and counselor are also not the solution.

The sixth approach is reliance on spiritual revival. Those who take this approach focus on prayers for revival and on the power of the gospel to bring about social change. The hope is for a miracle. The problem is not with this emphasis but with the dualism that is associated with it. It pits prayer against the lessons of the social sciences. God's spiritual work is pitted against the normative rules and dynamics of cultural change. If one believes that God is sovereign in history, as most Christian believers do, then this history includes the normal dynamics of culture. He is able to do miracles and bring revival when everything makes it seem unlikely. But one does not have to pit science against faith. God's miraculous healing can also be seen through the hands and skills of the medical doctor working within the normal dynamics of medical science. Effective spiritual effort in culture is never an

---

[7] Ibid. 32.
[8] George Lakoff and Mark Johnson. *Philosophy in the Flesh* (Basic Books, 1999), p. 13.
[9] Pierre Bourdieu. *The Logic of Practice* (Stanford University Press, 1990), p. 9.

either/or proposition. To suggest, as some have, that a concern for following the sociological rules of social change is in some way less spiritual than praying for revival or acknowledging the power of the gospel is unfair and unhelpful. These believers are being too spiritual by half. There is no need to put spirituality in opposition to social science or science. The unifying factor in these ineffective approaches toward cultural change is their reliance on individual action and change rather than the dense network.

## A Relational Reality

The emphasis of the individual over the group is a relatively new mode of thought in contemporary America. Historically the group had precedence over the individual. The deepest reason for this belief in the West was the belief in the Christian Trinity—Father, Son, and Holy Spirit. The one God was a plurality of persons suggesting that the deepest things of reality are personal and relational. Only recently have we come to see the liabilities of Western modernity in placing the importance of the individual over the group. Individualism is a troubling implication of the Enlightenment. Rohr laments, "What won out in our entire Western anthropology was human individuality and human rationality, instead of foundational relationally and an honoring of the intuitive nature of the human person, which is a healthy religion's natural habitat." [10] Theologically, historically, and sociologically the priority of the individual has never been held in such high esteem as today. Historically, there was always the priority of the social group over the lone individual; theologically, the Trinity and the church were placed over the autonomous self; and sociologically, it was the tribe and family that had a priority over the individual. This is not so today.

Today any infringement on the rights, autonomy, or freedom of the individual is a fundamental affront to what is prized and presumed to be the deepest truth of reality. In this view, identity and morality are infinitely pliable fictions that relate to nothing

---

[10] Richard Rohr. *The Divine Dance: The Trinity and Your Transformation* (Whitaker House, 2016), p. 74.

that is transcendent. It is reasonable to question the accuracy of these assumptions. It is not true to human anthropology or to the nature of reality. The truth is that each of us is a "*we*" before we are a "*me*." Long before we even know our name, we are born into a family with a family history. Spirituality was never intended to be "just Jesus and I me and Jesus." Historically, the spiritual person entered into an apprenticeship in a tradition —Buddhist, Hindu, Christian, or otherwise. For the Christians, the belief in a relational reality is ultimately grounded in the Trinity. The fact that the Trinity is a triad, not a binary, means that reality is never dualistic. The fact that the Trinity is personal, not impersonal, means that self-giving generative mutuality of love is at the heart of all that exists. This is a beautiful metaphysical truth that belies much of our contemporary practice. These views were central to ancient Orthodox and Celtic spirituality.

A similar understanding of reality is also acknowledged by Eastern religions. Hindu physician Deepak Chopra asks, "Are our genes verbs or nouns?" He continues, "There are no nouns in the universe. Everything is a relationship. Nouns are conventions of language. The universe is more music than words. The universe is a verb, a process of ceaseless activity."[11] Neuroscientist Iain McGilchrist reinforces Chopra's point, stating that in evolutionary development music leads to language, rather than language to music.[12] Likewise, many young people today eschew black and white thinking, gravitating instead to mystery, complexity, ambiguity, and shades of grey. They are three-dimensional thinkers, echoing the sensibility of artist Vincent van Gogh who said, "Life is probably round," or better, "spherical."[13] A relational reality is a networked reality.

It is only forms of contemporary evangelicalism as it has accommodated itself to Enlightenment individualism that does

---

[11] Deepak Chopra. "LIVE from The Nantucket Project," AOL Build video, 56:29, September 23, 2016, build.aol.com/video/57e55a845095495a4c595d0.

[12] Iain McGilchrist. *The Master and his Emissary: The Divided Brain and the Making of the Western World* (Yale, 2010), p. 105.

[13] Ibid., 448. See also Windrider Institute's assessment of spherical thinking: https://www.windriderforum.info/portfolio_page/episode-three-sphere-thinking/.

not prioritize the group over the individual, sociology over psychology, or church community over the individual convert. These believers may talk "*community*," but community is only a nice extra, not foundational, and certainly not considered essential to either conversion or discipleship. They may talk about the Reformation's priesthood of the believer without an equal appreciation for tradition, which is the ongoing respect for the community of the dead. [14] The accommodation to the individualism of modernity means that many faith-based communities have a soteriology without a matching ecclesiology. The inevitable logic of evangelical individualism is the "do-it-yourself spirituality" of the religious none that eschews a commitment to, respect for, or obligation to the other—in particular the institutional church. These views are coming under increasing critique today.[15] Individualism is increasingly deemed a problem. British theologian Lesslie Newbigin laments that, "The churches of Europe and their cultural offshoots in the Americas had largely come to a kind of comfortable cohabitation with the Enlightenment."[16] It is an ideology that many are coming to see that tells a distorted message about the nature of persons and reality. This critique is actually being extended from religion to science.

The Enlightenment taught us to see things in parts rather than as wholes. Notre Dame physicist Albert-László Barabási writes, "Reductionism was the driving force behind much of the twentieth-century's scientific research. The assumption is that once we understand the parts, it will be easy to grasp the whole." But this has proven to be a faulty premise. He continues, "Today we increasingly recognize that nothing happens in isolation. Most events and phenomena are connected, caused by, and interacting with a huge number of other pieces of a complex universal

---

[14] "Tradition means giving a vote to most obscure of all classes, our ancestors. It is the democracy of the dead." G.K. Chesterton. *Orthodoxy* (Image Books, 1959), p. 48.
[15] Conceicao Soares. "The Philosophy of Individualism: A Critical Perspective," *International Journal of Philosophy & Social Values*, June 2018.
[16] Lesslie Newbigin. *Proper Confidence: Faith, Doubt, & Certainty in Christian Discipleship* (Eerdmans, 1995), p. 33.

puzzle."[17] Contemporary thinking is resorting to a greater appreciation of the holistic organism or the ecosystem—the priority of the orchard over the apple. Sociologist James Hunter observes, "There is more to the apple than the apple itself; that to understand apples—how they grow, what makes a sweet-tasting apple from one that tastes like cardboard, and so on—one must understand as much as one can about the larger tree, about the soil that nourishes the roots of the tree, about the different climates that effect rainfall, sunshine, prevalence of bugs, insects and other pests."[18] The science of networks has emerged from this growing appreciation. Historic Christian orthodoxy as well as contemporary neuroscience and physics are all now reaffirming the priority of thinking of reality as an ecosystem, in effect as a functioning dense network. Spirituality has again joined ecology. What environmentalists assumed, others are now being forced to acknowledge.[19]

It will be impossible for the reader to have a sufficient appreciation for dense networks unless he or she, if a faith-based believer, restores a commitment to the Trinity as the heart of historic orthodoxy and if not a believer at least an appreciation of the ecosystem of nature and neurology. The substance of this book is not merely a pragmatic tool for organizational effectiveness, rather it is a reaffirmation of a *metaphysically relational reality*. Reality is a weblike universe. Barabási affirms, "By uncovering the mechanisms that govern network evolution, we have grasped the universality of the arsenal of tools nature uses to create the complex world around us."[20] Affirming the priority of the Trinity is reorienting our lives around what is most true about ourselves and the world. Dense networks are effective because they are true to reality. In traditional Christian terms, the Trinity is the *why* behind the *what* of dense networks. It is not just a good idea or a useful tool, it is the way reality works.

---

[17] Albert-Lászloó Barabási. *Linked: The New Science of Networks* (Perseus Publishing, 2002), p. 6, 7.
[18] James Davison Hunter, "Proem," unpublished manuscript, 2021.
[19] David Abram. *The Spell of the Sensuous* (Vintage Books, 1997).
[20] Ibid. 107.

If one is serious about making lasting social change, then the principles of social dynamics must be followed. There is an ontological basis for dense networks. Networks work because reality is relational. In contrast to society's emphasis on the individual, dense networks are the main actor in effective long-term social change. For those interested in leveraging their social impact, following the rules of social change is the necessary starting point. Anything else is doomed to failure.

## Social Dynamics Rule:

*The "why" behind the power of dense networks is that we live in a Trinitarian universe. Reality is essentially relational, a web-like network.*

# THE PICTURE
## Catalyst, Lever, Fulcrum, and World

*"All our truth, or all but a few fragments,*
*is won by metaphor."[21]*
– C.S. Lewis

We always think first in pictures. They serve as the frame through which we see everything else. We have to win the frame before arguing the facts. Cognitive scientist George Lakoff observes, "People think in frames…. To be accepted, the truth must fit people's frames. If the facts do not fit the frame, the frame stays and the facts bounce off."[22] Moreover, the frame dictates who we become. Iris Murdoch wrote, "Man is a creature who makes pictures of himself and then comes to resemble the picture."[23] Our lives are framed by our chosen frame.

I have acknowledged that the dense network frame is largely counter to the individualistic frame that dominates the West and has infused itself into American cultural and religious dispositions. So the aim of this book is to reframe a key aspect of the dynamics of cultural change through a simple picture: a lever, a fulcrum, and a world that collectively serve as the law of social leverage. We will look at each briefly here before discussing them in more detail later in subsequent chapters.

---

[21] C.S. Lewis.`` Bluspels and Flalansferes," *The Importance of Language*. ed. Max Black (Eaglewood Cliffs: Prentice-Hall, 1962), p. 50.
[22] George Lakoff. *Don't Think of an Elephant! Know Your Values and Frame the Debate* (Chelsea Green Publisher, 2014), p. 17.
[23] Iris Murdoch. "Metaphysics and Ethics," *Existentialists and Mystics* (Penguin Press, 1998), p. 75.

### The Catalyst

Dense networks do not happen by accident. They require a catalytic individual to launch the process. At one level, this seems to fly in the face of the general argument that social change is not up to the individual. But actually, in every case where dense networks have successfully made a lasting difference, there has been a catalytic individual or individuals to start the process. Somebody has to have the vision to start the process.

### The Lever

In this picture, the lever is a shared cause concept, the telos or ultimate object or aim of an individual's or organization's mission. For a network to organize, it needs to be about something that is personally meaningful and inspirational. Many organizations have a murky cause concept, which weakens its potential for leverage. This is particularly true for networks that seek to coalesce around a school of thought. If it is not simple, clear, and distinctive, then it is ineffective. One sees the power of simplicity in Martin Seligman's core concept for positive psychology. Everyone can appreciate a research shift from mental illness to mental health, from dysfunction to well-being. Einstein's wisdom applies to one's cause concept: "Everything should be made as simple as possible, but not simpler." Another version of the same idea is his "If you can't explain it to a six- year-old, you don't understand it yourself."[24] Every organization needs to determine whether they have an effective cause concept to serve as its lever. Clear and simple is best.

### The Fulcrum

The members of the dense network are the fulcrum that gives the cause concept a point of leverage. The network is the fulcrum. It is here that we discuss what constitutes an effective network. In the context of social media—such as Facebook and Twitter—this

---

[24] Andrew Robinson, "Did Einstein Really Say That?" *Nature,* April 30, 2018: https://www.nature.com/articles/d41586-018-05004-4/ and https://www.cambridgenetwork.co.uk/news/if-you-can-t-explain-it-to-a-six-year-old-you-probably-don-t4190/.

concept needs to be clarified. We all know from experience that a Facebook "friend" is not the same thing as a genuine friend forged through the ups and downs of life lived together face-to-face. A social affinity group—an alumni association, for example—is also not a dense network. The fact that a group of people come to a church does not make them an effective dense network. One of the immediate challenges of church leadership is knowing how to turn natural affinity associations into an effective dense network.

Moreover, a fulcrum has a dynamic interdependent ecology, one that includes both supporters and soldiers. Too often all of our attention is on the soldiers without equal attention paid to the lines of logistics. And often the supporters are not given a meaningful role in the soldiering. All of the stakeholders of a network need to function as in an interdependent ecology. It is only when all the stakeholders are aligned to the cause concept that maximum force can be applied to a given world.

## The World

Leverage only happens when there is a uniformity of vision around a singular cause concept that is addressing a specific, embodied, geographically-located world. The setup of the typical American evangelical church experience does not immediately lend itself to this focus on a specific world. Churches have aligned themselves with car culture. Many church members come from diverse and distant neighborhoods. They may see each other on Sunday mornings, but it is unlikely that in their day-to-day activities they will have opportunities to meet. They are Sunday friends and mid-week strangers. What we are seeing in the typical church is a "community" oriented to a plurality of worlds, but not to a single world. What is common in churches facilitated by automotive mobility rather than geographic proximity is a fragmentation of worlds.

Moreover, depending on the size of the church, the membership is itself divided among a host of competing interest groups. Some people may be loyally committed to their small group or to a Sunday school class, but not to the church as a whole.

"Community" as it is discussed and realized practically within most churches today is no more a real community than a Facebook "friend" is a real friend.

A community of people without a shared purpose, without unifying relational commitments and clarity of vision, without real relational conflict stemming from embodied proximity, without a focus on a particular world to be reached as a community... looks like most evangelical churches today. Is it any wonder that the church is losing its effectiveness within society? One's system is perfectly designed for the results one is achieving. In this case, church community has been designed for ineffectiveness in social impact.

Generally, there is a lack of clarity about what a church or organization is about and whom one is seeking to serve. Many churches have a lever problem and a world problem, which impacts the effectiveness of the fulcrum. If the lever, or the cause concept, bends, then there is no effective concentrated moment of force. If the lever is moved constantly so that it doesn't get purchase on one thing, then there is no effective moment of force.

So, with this unified picture going forward, we will examine the individual parts that will enhance your leverage or effective social impact: we will assess the strength and clarity of your lever, the density and commitments of your fulcrum, and the concreteness of your world.

We often talk the talk of wanting to create cultural change. It is now possible to walk the walk. Let's unpack this four-fold metaphor and reveal the laws of effective social leverage based on the best insights of network science.

## Social Dynamics Rule:

*We think first in pictures.*
*The essential picture of this book is*
*catalyst, lever, fulcrum, and world.*

# THE CATALYST

# CATALYTIC LEADERSHIP

*"When the best leader's work is done the people say,*
*'We did it ourselves.'"*[25]
— Lao Tzu

Readers may not immediately recognize the names of Patrisse Cullors, Alicia Garza, and Opal Tometi. They are the national co-founders of Black Lives Matter, a decentralized dense network of political activists who were first galvanized by the acquittal of Trayvon Martin's murderer, George Zimmerman, in 2013. Black Lives Matter aims to highlight the depth of brutality, injustice, and unaccountability that American society, especially law enforcement, harbors toward black people. The project is now a member-led global network of more than 40 chapters. Its members organize and build local power to intervene in violence inflicted on Black communities by the state and vigilantes. The point here is not to debate the policies and practices advocated by Black Lives Matter, but to observe the structure and dynamics of the organization's leadership. There are reasons why it has become such a powerful movement. There are lessons everyone can learn from their success.

While this network was formed by three Oakland-based Black feminists, the network's life and momentum is directed by its members, not its leaders. They state, "The Black Lives Matter Global Network is as powerful as it is because of our membership, our partners, our supporters, our staff, and you. Our continued commitment to liberation for all Black people means we are continuing the work of our ancestors and fighting for our collective freedom because it is our duty."[26] Its members matter now more than its leaders. The celebrity name most associated

---

[25] Lao Tzu, translated by Derek Lin. *Tao Te Ching* (Skylight Paths, 2006).
[26] https://blacklivesmatter.com/what-we-believe/.

with Black Lives Matter is Colin Kaepernick, the former NFL quarterback known for taking a knee in protest to police brutality during the singing of the national anthem at the beginning of NFL games.[27] Kaepernick has become the face of the new civil rights movement. On September 3, 2018, Labor Day 2018, Nike launched an ad featuring Colin Kaepernick, which became as controversial as Black Lives Matter and later won an Emmy for Outstanding Commercial. The Nike ad, "Dream Crazy," blended commerce with political activism and was a clarion call to make a difference with one's life.

*If people say your dreams are crazy*
*If they laugh at what you think you can do*
*Good*
*Stay that way*
*Because what non-believers fail to understand is*
      *that calling a dream crazy is not an insult*
*It's a complement*
*Don't try to be the fastest runner in your school*
*Or the fastest in the world*
*Be the fastest ever*
*Don't picture yourself wearing OBJ's jersey*
*Picture OBJ wearing yours*
*Don't settle for homecoming queen or linebacker*
*Do both*
*Lose 120 pounds and become an Ironman*
      *after beating a brain tumor*
*Don't believe you have to be like anybody to be somebody*
*If you're born a refugee, don't let that stop you from playing soccer*
*For the national team*
*At age 16*
*Don't become the best basketball player on the planet*
*Be bigger than basketball*

---

[27] Though my words don't mean much, it should be apparent that I stand with Kaepernick and believe that Black Lives Matter. Racism in all forms must end. Systemic racism is real and it too must end. This does not mean that I agree with all of Black Lives Matter's public actions or in Critical Race Theory.

*Believe in something, even if it means sacrificing everything*
*When they talk about the greatest team in the history of the sport,*
*make sure it's your team*
*If you have only one hand, don't just watch football*
*Play it*
*At the highest level*
*And if you're a girl from Compton,*
      *don't just become a tennis player*
*Become the greatest athlete ever*
*Yeah, that's more like it*
*So don't ask if your dreams are crazy*
*Ask if they're crazy enough.*[28]

Stephen Green, president of the People's Consortium, stated, "Kaepernick is a modern-day Rosa Parks and Muhammad Ali all in one."[29] He has become the face of the systemic racism of the NFL and a cause-celeb antagonist of President Trump. His own life story has served to illustrate and fuel the movement, but he was not its cause, nor does he have any ongoing leadership role within it.

It is a strength of Black Lives Matter not to have any high-profile leaders who would inevitably be the singular target of ongoing political and racial hatred. By being an amorphous movement of people-led chapters across the country they have the power of a network without the liabilities of a leader-led movement. They become much harder to attack collectively even while they mobilize collective action. The main point here is the organizational humility of the Black Lives Matter co-founders. This is a singular example of being a catalytic force without an attention demanding ego. With the murder of George Floyd and the wide-spread national protests that ensued, with public opinion finally swinging in favor of Black Lives Matter, we did not see

---

[28] https://theinspirationroom.com/daily/2019/nike-dream-crazy/.
[29] Jason Reid, "How Colin Kaepernick Became a Cause for Activists Civil Rights Groups," *The Undefeated*:
https://theundefeated.com/features/how-colin-kaepernick-became-a-cause-for-activists-civil-rights-groups/.

celebrity Black Lives Matter leaders take to the airwaves. Even at a moment of historic inflection, it was the people's voices that mattered, not its leaders. When Farhad Manjoo wrote a column in *The New York Times*, "Black Lives Matters Is Winning," not once did he quote a national Black Lives Matter leader.[30] I can think of few other dense networks where such would be the case. Can you imagine a faith-based social movement that has just garnered national attention and positive national support following in these same patterns of deference to the group over the individual? It is hard to imagine.

Dense networks do not happen by accident. They require a catalytic individual to launch the process. At one level this seems to fly in the face of the general argument that social change is not up to the individual. No, in every case where dense networks have successfully made a lasting difference, there has been a catalytic individual or individuals to start the process. Somebody has to have the vision to start the process. The *Stanford Social Innovation Review* finds, "Network entrepreneurs actively catalyze networks (or organizations that function like networks), leading to an exponential increase in growth and scale beyond what their own organization could accomplish. These leaders don't use a single approach, employ a single tool, or operate alone. As they expand and evolve their networks—far beyond the walls of their own organizations—they make sure that their own power fades and the capacity of others grows."[31] This person is often afforded the deference of being the face of the movement, its tacit leader. Yet to the degree that a dense network is focused on a solitary leader rather than on the shared desires of the group who are collectively aligned to a specific cause, to that degree the dense network will eventually fail. A dense network requires a catalytic network leader. So the irony is that the main actor on the stage of social change is the dense network, but the dense network demands the

---

[30] Farhad Manjoo, "Black Lives Matter Is Winning," The New York Times, June 10, 2020: https://www.nytimes.com/2020/06/10/opinion/black-lives-matter-protests.html/.

[31] https://ssir.org/network_entrepreneurs/. See also Jerry Toomer. *The Catalyst Effect: 12 Skills and Behaviors to Boost Your Impact and Elevate Team Performance* (Emerald Publishing Limited, 2018).

intentionality of a visionary, collaborative leader who is willing to immediately fade back into the identity and momentum of the group. Such leadership is as necessary as it is rare.

This illustrates the fact that dense networks need a catalytic beginning by an individual or individuals—they do not happen on their own—but the significance of the dense network is not the organizer/s as much as the network itself. This leader sees the issue, brings visibility to the issue and empowers the people in the network around this issue by giving direction but not holding power over the people in the network. This combination of charismatic vision and deferential collaborative humility is a rare quality in organizational leaders but is a requirement of effective social leverage.

## Social Dynamic Rule:

*Dense networks require an animating visionary catalytic leader who is willing at the same time to return authority to the dense network.*

# THE ABOLITIONIST NETWORK
## The Clapham Circle

*"Historian John Pollack has written that Wilberforce's
life is proof that a man can change his
times, though he cannot do it alone."[32]*
— Kevin Belmonte

We now turn to a prime example of a dense network to illustrate
the catalyst, the lever, the fulcrum, and the world. The case study
that has garnered the most attention among Washington
Christians is the Clapham Circle, the knights-of-the-round-table
paradigm of dense networks. Historian Belmonte states, "Their
legacy offers the best model we have for turning around a society
and culture."[33] The Clapham Circle—sometimes referred to as the
Clapham Sect or lampooned as "the saints"—was an informal
group of aristocratic evangelical Anglicans associated
professionally and relationally with William Wilberforce, many of
whom lived in the suburban village of Clapham about four miles
south from the center of London from about 1790 to 1830.

Historical discussions about the significance of this group tend to
be overshadowed by biographical adulation of William
Wilberforce. Contemporary commentators stated that
Wilberforce was, "the very sun of the Clapham system." [34]
Historical accounts have a way of celebrating the individual
because it is a story so much easier to tell in book and film than
the story of a complex network of overlapping friends and family.
All that being said, Wilberforce cast a large shadow over the

---

[32] Kevin Belmonte. *Hero for Humanity: A Biography of William Wilberforce* (NavPress, 2002), p. 175.
[33] Ibid. 151.
[34] William Hague. *William Wilberforce: The Life of the Great Anti-Slave Trade Campaigner* (Harcourt, 2007), p. 220.

Clapham community and its informal dense network. It is certainly true that discussions about this group can feel like an ahistorical reification of actual reality. One can make it appear to be a much more organized, self-conscious, and mobilized group than it really was. It was a dense network that grew naturally, almost spontaneously, in the midst of life lived together. But there are important lessons to be learned here from a particular dense network that made a lasting historical cultural difference, namely the abolition of slavery in England in 1833. The Clapham Circle demonstrates the social changing potential of dense networks.

But in the telling, one must acknowledge that actual life is less clear cut and more messy and murky than it is typically described in historical accounts that gloss over the complexities of human motivations and intertwined relationships. From the hindsight of 200 years and 30,000 feet, one can tend to make historical examples prove any point one wants to make. So in the telling of this story, my conclusion of whether it was Wilberforce (the individual) or his circle of friends (the dense network) that made the most difference is that it is both. Networks need a catalytic leader.

The female counterpart to Wilberforce was the playwright and writer Hannah More. Karen Prior acknowledges that, "More was the mastermind behind some of the abolitionist movement's more effective campaigns to sway public opinion."[35] In our picture, Wilberforce served as the catalyst and the Clapham Circle the fulcrum. They needed each other.

### Spontaneity and Close Proximity
The Clapham Circle was not a self-conscious dense network. Though it was recognized at the time as a gathering of influential evangelicals, it was only after the death of Wilberforce that the network took on a formal identity in retrospective hagiography. It was first called *"The Clapham Sect"* in a book of church history in

---

[35] Karen Swallow Prior. *Fierce Convictions: The Extraordinary Life of Hannah More—Poet, Reformer, and Abolitionist* (Thomas Nelson, 2014), p. 133.

1844, a decade after Wilberforce's death.[36] So the first lesson is that a dense network can form spontaneously for a variety of overlapping reasons. Rarely do they form self-consciously as a conscious strategy of cultural influence.

Perhaps the modern-day equivalent of the Clapham Circle is the dense network that formed around Dr. Francis Schaeffer and those influenced by Swiss L'Abri. The ongoing connections of L'Abri loom large through thought leaders like Os Guinness, Steven Garber, David Gill, Robert Kramer, Bill Edgar, Mark Ryan, Denis Haack, Skip Ryan, David Wells, Vishal Mangalwadi, Udo Middlemann, Ranald Macaulay, and Jerram Barrs. [37] Historian Charles Cotherman writes, "The relational network that L'Abri forged still exerted significant influence within American life decades after Francis Schaeffer's death."[38]

It is not totally clear who first conceived of forming a "colony of like-minded people" in and around the Clapham Common.[39] Henry Thornton, first cousin of Wilberforce and wealthy businessman, first purchased a large home there, Battersea Rise, and later expanded it into a 34-bedroom mansion with numerous guest houses surrounding it. This home had a grand oval library that served as the informal gathering place for conversation and fellowship. Battersea Rise served as Highclere Castle does in Downton Abbey as the physical center of the Clapham Circle.

In addition, the local rector, Henry Venn, who had been brought to Clapham by Henry Thornton to infuse more evangelical preaching into Holy Trinity Church, the Anglican church in Clapham, was himself eager to build the size and influence of his congregation. His son, John, eventually took over the parish.

---

[36] Sir James Stephen. *Essays in Ecclesiastical Biography.* Volumes I-II (Longmans, 1849).
[37] See Charles E. Cotherman. *To Think Christianly: A History of L'Abri, Regent College, and the Christian Study Center Movement* (InterVarsity Academic, 2020). This book describes the scope of L'Abri's influence within American evangelicalism and frames it as a network of relationships.
[38] Ibid. 46.
[39] Hague, p. 217.

And finally, there was the larger-than-life celebrity politician William Wilberforce who eventually decided to settle there with his new bride in 1770. Clapham was not exactly a gated community, but it does have the feel of the Kennedy compound in Hyannis, Massachusetts. What is significant here is the proximity of friends and frequency of conversations it afforded in a world before telephones and the Internet.

## High Sociality

The character of the dense network goes beyond neighborly proximity. These were long established elite college friendships with major associations stemming from St. Edmund Hall at Oxford University and Magdalene College at Cambridge University, similar to the alumni associations and secret societies of Harvard, Yale, and Princeton. Galvanizing these friendships was a shared evangelical Anglicanism that was looked down upon by others within the British upper class. This shared class stigma served as a bonding negative force for this group of friends. But the most important factor in the Clapham Circle was intermarriage. This was a complex web of overlapping family ties where everyone was related to someone else within the group by blood or marriage. Author Eric Metaxas elaborates:

> As we have seen, Henry Thornton was Wilberforce's cousin; Gisborne married Babington's sister; and Babington married Macaulay's sister. In addition, Charles Eliot married John Venn's sister; James Stephen married Wilberforce's sister; and, all available sisters having been taken, Macaulay married a pupil of Hannah More. Soon, too, the next generation added its ties, and the son of James Stephen married the daughter of John Venn.[40]

One of the casualties of modernity and mobility is this lack of proximate, embedded, aligned friendships. Wilberforce would

---

[40] Eric Metaxas. *Amazing Grace: William Wilberforce and the Heroic Campaign to End Slavery* (HarperSanFrancisco, 2007), p. 187. One also gets a sense of this complex family web from Ernest Howe's book, *Saints in Politics: The 'Clapham Sect' and the Growth of Freedom* (George Allen & Unwin, 1960).

have understood C.S. Lewis's sentiment, "Friendship is the greatest of worldly goods…. If I had to give a piece of advice to a young man about a place to live, I think I should say, 'sacrifice almost everything to live where you can be near your friends.'"[41] Clapham provided just such a place. Wilberforce knew that his friendships were one of the most important parts of his life and were indispensable to his effectiveness. Clapham was a place infused with relational sociality. The dynamic between these friends was informal, familial, and lubricated with shared meals and long talks. If ever there was a dense network in Antonio Gramsci's sense of "organic intellectuals," it was the Clapham Circle. Organic intellectuals are not academic scholars, but partisan activists—they have a definite point of view, are pragmatically oriented to daily life instead of abstractions, and are frequently common workers. They are doers more than just thinkers.[42]

**Access to Cultural Capital**
This brings us to the composition of the Clapham Circle. This was a network of wealthy, accomplished, and influential upper class evangelical Anglicans. They are the kind of people who today would regularly attend the annual Aspen Ideas Festival, TED Talks, The Nantucket Project, and would have memberships in the Yale and Harvard Clubs. Historian Kevin Belmonte writes, "It was a brilliant circle, counting among its members poet, play-wright, and educational reformer Hannah More, abolitionist pioneer Granville Sharp, the gifted lawyer James Stephen, and Zachary Macaulay. All had embraced the life-changing faith that had transformed Wilberforce's life, and they sought to love God and promote the happiness of their fellow-creatures as he did."[43] James Davison Hunter adds, "It was well known too that Wilberforce was not an isolated actor but was surrounded and supported by a network of friends, associates, and sympathizers….

---

[41] C.S. Lewis. *The Letters of C.S. Lewis to Arthur Greeves* (Collier Books, 1986), p. 477.
[42] Antonio Gramsci. See "The Intellectuals" in *Selections from the Prison Notebooks*. Translated and Edited by Q. Hoare and G. N. Smith. (International Publishers, 1971), page 3-23.

[43] Belmonte, p. 179.

One can count over two dozen leaders from the highest echelons of business, church, literary life, and government and politics who were connected and worked together in common cause. These individuals either came from or operated within the centers of cultural influence. The majority were exceptionally well educated." [44] Notable in the makeup of the group was their combination of professional diversity and social prominence. This was not just a group of idealist activist politicians or progressive ministers. Rather it was an eclectic group that included a playwright, philanthropists, educators, a brewer, a mathematician, clergymen, glassmaker, politicians, writers, and bankers. Social reformer Hannah More described the group as a virtual "Noah's ark, full of beasts, clean and unclean."[45]

## Their Lever

Over time, the Clapham Circle came to be associated with the abolition of slavery. It was a major social issue of the day and there were committed abolitionists counted among its members. So it was not just an externalization of William Wilberforce's sense of calling. Even more than their belief in abolition was a sense animated by a shared evangelical faith that they had to use their sources of influence to make the world a better place. They believed that a heart and life dedicated to social justice is the inevitable sign of real faith as stated in James 1:27—"Religion that God our Father accepts pure and faultless is this: to look after orphans and widows in their distress and to keep oneself from being polluted by the world" (NIV). Over the course of the following 40 years, they started or were active in over 200 nonprofit social service endeavors. But clearly the animating center of their concern was slavery.

Few today recognize how intertwined the British economy was with slavery at that time. Working for the abolition of slavery as a social issue is like campaigning today to abandon the internal

---

[44] Hunter, p. 73.
[45] Prior, p. 173.

combustion engine or to enact the Green New Deal. It was an audacious goal that took political patience and cultural creativity.

They were aware that politics was downstream from culture and adopted strategies that were the first large scale public relations campaign. It is unlikely that this issue could have sustained momentum without a dense network behind it. It was only days before Wilberforce's death in 1833 that slavery was finally abolished in the British Empire after an almost 40-year campaign. This was a generational project.

No one stopped to strategize how they should create a dense network in order to influence the abolition of slavery. No: in this case, there was a spontaneous serendipitous synergy of factors that came together to create a powerful and effective dense network. They had multiple catalysts (Thornton, Venn, Wilberforce, and More). They had a unifying cause concept, the abolishment of slavery in the British Empire. And they had a dense network with a high degree of sociality and solidarity. They were able to focus their efforts on the cause in both the cultural arena (more on this later) as well as the political one in a manner that created lasting social change. With the principal cause completed and their galvanizing catalyst dead, the network slowly dissolved as one might expect after 1833.

The Clapham Circle was not a dense network that endured or was able to successfully transmit its values to the succeeding generations. There is a warning here in that dense networks can be used both for social good and decay. Wilberforce's eldest son, William, never embraced faith. This is a shared situation that many church and faith-based leaders face personally. And the grandchildren of many of the leaders of the Clapham Circle (More, Macaulay, Stephens, Thornton, and Wilberforce) were active leaders in the libertine literary intellectual network known as the Bloomsbury Group. [46] Historian of American change

---

[46] Christopher Tolley. *Domestic Biography: The Legacy of Evangelicalism in Four Nineteenth-Century Families*
(Clarendon Press, 1997).

Gertrude Himmelfarb notes, "Bloomsbury was, in fact, as much a group (or circle) as Clapham was a sect. And it performed something of the same function, setting the tone and agenda for the cultural 'vanguard' of the nation. Where Clapham had inspired a moral and spiritual reformation, Bloomsbury sought to effect a moral and spiritual liberation—a liberation from Clapham itself and from the vestiges of evangelicalism and Victorianism that still persisted in the early 20th century."[47] The social dynamic of Bloomsbury was not intermarriage but overlapping affairs. Dorothy Parker said of Bloomsbury, "They lived in squares, painted in circles, and loved in triangles."[48]

While this is a sad legacy of the Clapham Circle, it continues to prove the wider point on the power of dense networks as an influential vehicle of social change for better or worse. Himmelfarb concludes about Bloomsbury, "It was because they were so conspicuously a group that they were able to find an 'adversary culture' strong enough to challenge the bourgeois culture."[49] Once again dense networks are proved to be the main actors on the stage of cultural change.

---

[47] Gertrude Himmelfarb. "From Clapham to Bloomsbury: A Genealogy of Morals," *Commentary*, February 1985:
https://www.commentarymagazine.com/articles/gertrude-himmelfarb/from-clapham-to-bloomsbury-a-genealogy-of-morals/.
[48] "All the Couples Were Triangles and Lived in Squares":
https://quoteinvestigator.com/2018/05/16/triangles/.
[49] Himmelfarb.

# THE LEVER

# THE TELOS

*"A cause concept is what a network thinks its efforts will produce in terms of outcomes. It answers the question of what they think their efforts will accomplish."[50]*
— *Ron Frey*

Dense networks can be large and small—a family group, missional colleagues, church community, political party, or a standing army. In each case, they need to be unified in what they are fundamentally about. They need a clear cause concept or *telos*.

The contrast between the abolitionist movement in England and the U.S. demonstrate the problem of not having a clear cause concept. In England, it was clear. In the U.S., murky at best.

History is rarely lived in black and white categories. It is normally murky from the start. Competing goals and motivations often make organizational unity and clarity of a cause concept difficult. How else do you reconcile that President Abraham Lincoln asked Colonel Robert E. Lee to command the Union Army at the outset of the Civil War? The highest-ranking U.S. general, Winfried Scott, advised President Lincoln to put Lee in command of the Union Army. Colonel Robert E. Lee ignored a Confederate offer of command, and Lincoln promoted him to major general.

Lee wasn't a strong believer in the Confederate cause. He was politically indifferent and considered secession to be a very unwise decision. In fact, he even privately ridiculed the Confederate "revolution" as a betrayal of the U.S. Constitution. Lee was also personally opposed to slavery, though he believed that the African American slaves were better off living in the USA than in Africa

---

[50] Ron Frey. *Find, Win, Keep, Life: Developing Donors for Life* (Frey Resource Group, 2020).

and thought that slavery would end when God willed it. As it turned out, Lee's primary loyalty was to his family and the state of Virginia. When Virginia joined the Confederacy on April 17, 1961, Lee reluctantly abandoned command of the Union Army, and resigned his commission on April 20. Three days later, he accepted the command of the Confederate Army of Northern Virginia.[51]

In hindsight, we tend to read history in binary categories. But rarely is that how history is actually lived. The U.S. Civil War was started with a host of conflicting motivations and rationales even by the principals involved. It was not until the third year of the war that Lincoln made slavery the issue of the war with the signing of the "Emancipation Proclamation" on January 1, 1863. But by then, the overarching sentiment in the North was simply ending the war and preserving the Union—slavery was no longer a major consideration even in the North.

This murkiness of the telos of the Civil War stands in direct contrast to the clarity of the British abolitionist movement that preceded it. British abolitionists were unequivocal at the outset of their campaign that abolishing slavery in the British Empire was the goal. This eventually took a two-step process: first abolishing the slave trade in 1807 and finally abolishing slavery itself in 1833. The U.S "Emancipation Proclamation" effectively kept the British from siding with the Confederacy, which Lincoln feared and was likely. Even the expediency of this military decision serves to diminish the clarity of the abolition of slavery as the overarching cause of the war. It is one thing to dispute over the power of the national government to prohibit slavery in the territories that had not yet become states and quite another to affirm the unequivocal evil of slavery itself. One is a process dispute; the other a dispute of fact, even moral turpitude.

It is merely historical conjecture what might have happened if the "Emancipation Proclamation" had been stated immediately after

---

[51] h ttps://history.info/did-you-know/general-lee-offered-command-union-army/.

the first shots were fired at Fort Sumter in April 1861. So it was that Reconstruction quickly gave way to the Jim Crow era and the murkiness of the Civil War became institutionalized in the South. It is said that the North won the war, but the South the myth surrounding it. The narrative of the "Lost Cause of the Confederacy" emerged, the American pseudo-historical, negationist ideology that holds that the cause of the Confederacy during the American Civil War was a just and heroic one.[52] The emergence of this myth is only possible in the context of a murky initial cause concept and the political ambivalence of the Andrew Johnson presidency, and the impotence of Reconstruction. The U.S. Civil War was fought with a murky cause concept. The contemporary conflict over Civil War monuments and the renaming of military bases named for Confederate generals after the Civil War is the continuing legacy of this historical murkiness and a legacy of the Jim Crow compromise.

In our four-fold metaphor—catalyst, lever, fulcrum, and world— the lever is the specific cause or issue that one wants to change. There is no meaningful cultural change without a clearly defined cause concept. At first blush this might seem obvious, but this is where many churches and organizations fail. It was a singular failure of Lincoln's leadership. What is the main point of your church or organization? Is it diffuse and ill defined? In some cases, we hint at our telos in our mission statement. A diffuse cause concept will not adequately serve as an institutional lever for lasting cultural change.

Your cause concept is not your mission statement or summary statement of what you do. Your cause concept is what you seek to produce, or the end purpose of an effort. It is a description of an effect desired, not the means to an effect. One's lever or cause concept should be able to be described in a clear simple picture of the outcomes of one's effort. It should be intuitively self-evident,

[52] David W. Blight. "Europe in 1989, America in 2020, and the Death of the Lost Cause," *The New Yorker*, July 1, 2020: https://www.newyorker.com/culture/cultural-comment/europe-in-1989-america-in-2020-and-the-death-of-thelost-cause/.

not the result of an extensive public relations campaign. It should need no argument. It must paint an unmistakably clear picture of one's intentions.

Your cause concept establishes the value proposition of your organization. It clarifies your competitive position vis-a-vis other competitors. In short, it is a picture of the difference you are seeking to make or the telos of your organization. If this is not clear or self-evident, then this is where the work must begin.

A cause concept must answer the question: What difference will you make? It is what unifies the emerging network being created. Cause concepts and branding are related, but different. Branding is related to marketing, communicating one's identity to a wide audience. But they are not totally unrelated. Retail consultant Jason Parkin notes, "It shouldn't come as a surprise that the power of purpose is increasingly important for both brands and consumers. In fact, 76 percent of millennials and Gen Z consumers say that they would pay more for a sustainable product, with 85 percent saying that sustainability influences their decision to purchase, even if it isn't their primary motivator."[53]

Increasingly brands need to be associated with causes that matters. A cause concept is about mobilizing a network of like-minded people. The outdoor clothing manufacturer Patagonia does this successfully by using their brand to create a network of environmental activists. "We aim to use the resources we have— our voice, our business and our community—to do something about our climate crisis. Join us and get involved."[54] Branding answers: "What kinds of goods and services do this company offer?" The cause concept answers: "What are the ends that those goods and services seek to create?"

---

[53] Jason Parkin, How Brands Can Build Loyalty in the Era of the Millennial and Gen Z," *Total Retail*, July 7, 2020:
https://www.mytotalretail.com/article/how-brands-can-build-loyalty-in-the-era-of-the-millennial-and-gen-z/.
[54] See https://www.patagonia.com/activism/.

## Creating a Cause Concept

When crafting a cause concept, it should be both simple and concrete. One should avoid abstractions. This point needs to be emphasized particularly for academic and public policy institutions that are seeking to create a school of thought or promote a particular worldview. Abstractions narrow and weaken the concept's appeal. It is sometimes necessary to focus on a concrete aspect of one's cause. Rescue missions have found great success in focusing their funding efforts around providing a single Thanksgiving meal for a homeless family in contrast to the broader, vaguer concept of solving the overarching homelessness problem. The goal is to link your cause concept to something concrete, something appealing, something other-directed, and something enduring. Wilberforce broke down his anti-slavery appeal to stop using sugar in your tea, as sugar production was associated with slavery. By making sugar consumption used in one's daily cup of tea associated with slavery; he changed the consciousness of a generation. In British society slavery was an abstraction. By making it about sugar in one's tea, the abolitionists made it concrete in the lives of British citizens. Hannah More penned this poem anonymously in a Bristol newspaper in 1792:

> I own I am shocked at this purchase of slaves,
> And fear those who buy them and sell them are knaves:
> What I hear of their hardships, their tortures and groans,
> Is almost enough to draw pity from stones.
> I pity them greatly, but I must be mum,
> For how could we do without sugar and rum?
> Especially, sugar, so needful we see,
> What, give up our desserts, our coffee, and tea?[55]

Also needed in a cause concept is the intensity associated with it and whether it will appeal to one's network for a long time. A controversial cause concept narrows the appeal, but increases the intensity, and increases the duration. A crisis cause concept—a

---

[55] Prior, p. 126.

natural disaster or pandemic—increases the intensity but decreases its duration. Needed is both intensity and duration. It is not surprising that the Clapham Circle largely disbanded after the abolition of slavery in 1833.

A church or nonprofit organization needs to frame its existence in terms of a specific cause concept. Ideally, this concept needs to be concrete, broadly appealing, and enduring. The reason that a cause concept is so important is that it is the central rationale for creating a network of likeminded individuals. The clearer this is defined in terms of the ends one is seeking to achieve, the more leverage one will achieve. Failure at this point is common. To get one's cause concept right, one must first win the frame so that one can successfully define reality.

## Social Dynamics Rule:

*There is no meaningful cultural dynamic without a clearly defined cause concept.*
*One's lever or cause concept should be able to be described in a clear simple picture of the outcomes of one's effort.*

# WINNING THE FRAME
## Moving Others to See with New Eyes

*"Just speaking truth to power doesn't work.*
*You need to frame the truths effectively*
*from your perspective."*[56]
— George Lakoff

In a pluralistic society, people hold diverse views. They articulate these views through diverse frames. These frames represent the underlying assumptions one's make about the nature of reality. When divergent frames are not recognized, people talk past each other. They may attempt to mount up facts from their perspective, but if the facts don't fit the alternative frame, the facts will bounce off and the frame will stay. Central to an effective implementation of a cause concept is winning the frame.

Discussions about sex are a relevant case in point. People have divergent frames when it comes to sexuality. Consequently, most of the traditional do's and don'ts of sexual ethics make no sense to them. Most of the church's talk about sexuality assumes a traditional frame, so traditional facts no longer make sense to young people who have adopted a nontraditional frame. We are at best talking past each other if not furthering the antagonism with our apparent moralism. The Korean expression of this is, "East question, West answer."[57]

State University of New York sociologist Steven Seidman explores these competing frames in his article, "Contesting the Moral

---

[56] George Lakoff. "11 Things Progressives Can Do": https://quizlet.com/77686602/lakoff-11-things-progressives-can-do-flash-cards/.
[57] http://koreanwithjohn.blogspot.com/2012/07/west-question-east-answer.html/.

Boundaries of Eros."[58] Americans, he writes, are divided between two different moral logics or frames when it comes to intimacy: the "morality of the sex act" logic and the "communicative sexual ethic" logic. "In the former," he writes, "sex acquires a determinative moral and social meaning as part of a cosmology, which may be understood in the language of religion, natural law, or secular reason.... By contrast, a communicative sexual ethic assumes that sex acts have no inherent meaning but gain their moral coherence from their interactive context."[59]

In the first frame, sex is a part of a larger cosmological world of meaning, it has an ontological basis in reality. Mila Kunis commented on her film *Friends with Benefits*, "Having friends with benefits is a lot like communism. It works well in theory, but not so well in execution."[60] It's a practice that is not aligned cosmologically with reality. Think of the morality ethic frame as sex as *cosmos*.

In the second frame, sex has no larger meaning beyond the consent to two participating adults. Here sexuality, though intrinsically embodied, is assumed to be disconnected from reality. It's a choice that doesn't touch the cosmos. The fact that sex is more like gravity is denied. Here sex has no larger "*why?*" Think of communicative ethic frame as sex as *consent*. It is clear that the communicative sexual frame legitimizes a much wider range of sexual practices that challenge the dominant morality ethic frame.

Christopher West is the leading popularizer of Pope John Paul II's "Theology of the Body." He gave a talk at the University of Pennsylvania to a group of LGBTQ activists on sexuality. By his own admission, it didn't go very well. I asked him if he gave his typical presentation: Desire, Design, and Destiny. He said that he

---

[58] Neil J. Smelser and Jeffrey C. Alexander, edited. *Diversity and Its Discontents: Cultural Conflict and Common Ground in Contemporary American Society* (Princeton University Press, 1999).
[59] Ibid. 168.
[60] David Marchese. "And She's Funny Too: A GQ&A with Mila Kunis," *Gentlemen Quarterly,* July 12, 2011: https://www.gq.com/story/mila-kunis-gq-august-2011-cover-story/.

did. "Where did you get hung up?" I asked. "Design," he answered. I said, "Yes, I'm not surprised, because you didn't win the frame first. Try giving a talk that is only about Desire and Destiny." He did this later at Eastern University and by doing so he framed sexuality as pointing to heaven and aligned to the cosmos. What was interesting is that once the topic was framed from this assumption the audience went on to say that this means this and that about its design—without any input from West. Winning the frame means everything. This often means needing to back up and define terms like "*reality*" that can no longer be taken for granted.

What is really at issue here is not this or that sexual practice, but the underlying meaning of sex itself, its framing assumptions. To argue the practice of sexuality without addressing the frame through which it is to be understood is a futile strategy. The point here is that unless you address the framing presuppositions, you are not addressing the core issue in a meaningful manner. To have cultural influence, your lever or cause concept must address the underlying frame. Otherwise, the effort is moot.

## Cause Concept as Metaphor

Ideally, the content of your cause concept is captured in a picture or a simple metaphor. Metaphors are the way we frame reality. Metaphors in this sense are not just a rhetorical flourish, but the way we use language to structure our experience of reality. Professors George Lakoff and Mark Johnson write, "Our conceptual systems thus play a central role in defining our everyday realities. If we are right in suggesting that our conceptual system is largely metaphorical, then the way we think, what we experience, and what we do every day is very much a matter of metaphor."[61] Philosopher of science Thomas Kuhn adds, "What a man sees depends both upon what he looks at and also upon what his previous visual-conceptual experience has taught him to see."[62]

---

[61] George Lakoff and Mark Johnson. *Metaphors We Live By* (University of Chicago Press, 1980), p. 3.
[62] Thomas Kuhn. *The Structures of Scientific Revolutions* (University of Chicago Press, 1970), p. 113.

Truth is won by metaphor.[63] Metaphors are language pictures that reveal our frame on reality.

Using metaphors effectively does three things: they challenge, open, and reveal. They challenge the older way of seeing reality and in doing so create the opportunity for us to do a "doggie head tilt." When dogs tilt their heads, some experts believe they are adjusting their pinnae, or outer ears, in order to better pinpoint the location of a noise. It means that you have gotten their attention. They are now listening attentively. Metaphors get our attention—they break the flow of the expected.

This new attention also activates one's imagination to think in creative new ways. When Jesus advised his followers to be, "as shrewd as snakes and as innocent as doves" (Matthew 10:16), he was giving wise rhetorical advice. Speak in a manner that does not create a defensive reaction to one's listeners and do so with an awareness of the appropriateness of timing. In short, be empathetic to your listener in your speech. Arguments that first engage reason narrow the scope of the conversation. Pictures or metaphors engage the imagination and open the scope of the conversation in fresh ways. Consider the metaphor written by American writer Mason Cooley, "A skyscraper is a boast in glass and steel."[64] If one changes the observation into an analogy, one can say, "A skyscraper is in architecture as a boast is in interpersonal relations." One should note that it is not literally true. Mardy Grothe affirms that one of the powers of metaphors is their ability to go beyond logic. "All metaphors are violations of logic in the sense that they assert that two different things are the same."[65] They demand a cognitive leap of faith. Thomas Kuhn in speaking of scientific paradigm shifts spoke of it in terms of "conversion." "Before they can hope to communicate fully, one

---

[63] Walter Hooper, edited. *Selected Literary Essays by C.S. Lewis* (Cambridge University Press, 1969), p. 265.
[64] Mardy Grothe. *i never metaphor i didn't like* (Collins, 2008), p. 7.
[65] Ibid. 8.

group or the other must experience the conversion that we have been calling a paradigm shift."[66]

It is this openness to a trans-rational (note: not non-rational) leap of faith that enable the listener to consider a new take on reality— a reframe—in a manner that is memorable. You'll probably never look at a skyscraper again without recalling this metaphor. Challenge, openness, reveal. We think first in pictures or metaphors. They in turn frame our perception of reality. We live in a cross-pressured world where people are operating with different frames. So we live in a world where people live with different perceptions of reality. The potential for conflict between frames is inevitable. It is for this reason that any effort at influencing culture must take into consideration first the importance of frames and second what a frame shift demands in terms of one's rhetorical strategy, namely the engagement of the imagination.

This is the controversial genius of Donald Trump's use of Tweets. George Lakoff argues that Trump's Tweets are an exercise in framing and are not to be parsed as a series of factual propositions. They are tactical rather than substantive. Because the news media is addicted to the latest "Breaking News," media companies rush to report on Trump's latest Tweet thereby playing directly into his hand. Trump uses Tweets to frame his ideas. Even when the media disagrees with the Tweet, they are inadvertently addressing their disagreement within the frame of Trump's choosing. Consider an example from January 7, 2017: "Only reason the hacking of the poorly defended DNC is discussed is that the loss by the Dems was so big that they are totally embarrassed." His goal was to shift the conversation off of Russian culpability to DNC negligence. Undefended, sloppy handling of classified information, deleted emails, questionable IT consultants were the reasons the DNC was hacked. This is an exercise in framing the facts ahead of time. Trump is in the framing business. He is a

---

[66] Kuhn, p. 150.

genius in shifting the conversation onto a frame of his choosing. Whoever wins the frame, wins the argument. This is why Lakoff, a Democratic strategist, pleads with the media not to engage with Trump's Tweets.

In addition, if you don't address the underlying assumptions that are expressed in a frame, you will inevitably lose the debate because you have not tackled the animating presuppositions. Once the political controversy of England leaving the European Union was framed as "*Brexit*," it is hardly surprising that those wanting to *exit* won the referendum. Rhetorical framing matters, because, as we know, if the facts don't fit the frame, the fact bounce off and the frame stays.[67] In matters of public debate and cultural change, frames rule. There is a tendency to argue over secondary matters rather than tackling the underlying assumptions. We need a cause concept strategy that addresses frames and the requirements of frame shifts. Otherwise, the lever of our dense network will not gain traction in a particular world.

### Seeing with "New Eyes"

Wilberforce knew that his significant political efforts on behalf of the abolition of slavery would not be adequate to change society. The Clapham Circle consequently developed a campaign, using media and the arts among other methods, to inform and change the consciousness of the nation. To this end, they used newspaper reports, boycotts, medallions, and posters. Of great significance was them showing a kneeling slave in chains in a supplicating posture asking, "Am I not a man and a brother?" Designed and manufactured by the celebrity pottery-maker Josiah Wedgwood, it became a high-end fashion statement. "Simply but brilliantly conceived, this image appealed to Christian compassion and Enlightenment ideas of equality while giving fashionable ladies and gentlemen the opportunity to demonstrate that they shared in these virtuous notions."[68] By making this a fashionable symbol of

---

[67] Lakoff, p. 17.
[68] Hague, p. 150.

"virtue-signaling," Wedgwood's medallion further engaged the social imagination of England.

The lesson here is that pictures win frames where arguments fail. Mike Metzger of The Clapham Institute writes, "Clapham believed human beings have the capacity to care about the suffering of others. They felt exposing suffering through the arts would move people to action. It worked. One historian attributed Clapham's success to how it 'evoked the conscience of the British people.'"[69] Proust captured this when he stated, "The real voyage of discovery lies not in finding new lands, but in seeing with new eyes."[70] "Seeing with new eyes" is the goal of a frame-shifting lever in service to cultural change.

The key to seeing with new eyes is to tell a better story through the use of the arts. Engaging the imagination requires framing one's cause concept in a story. Whoever tells a better, more compelling story wins. This is the repeated lesson of history. Jonah Sachs states in *Winning the Story Wars*,

> Where there is power, there is struggle for it. That's why, just below the surface, just beyond what the uninitiated can see, there are wars going on. The soldiers are Tea Party demonstrators and champions of "the 99 percent," climate change activists, makers of computers and sneaker brands. They seem to be fighting over ideas and dollars, but they are really fighting for control of our stories. The best of them, those who know this and can convince us that their story is true, are blowing everyone else to smithereens.[71]

Stories on steroids are myths. These are stories that tap into the collective unconscious. Alexandr Solzhenitsyn, the Nobel Prize winning novelist and political activist, believed that stories are

---

[69] Mike Metzger. "Fiction, Fables, & Stories," *The Clapham Commentary*: https://claphaminstitute.org/fictionfables-stories/. Adam Hochschild, *Bury The Chains: Prophets and Rebels in the Fight to Free an Empire's Slaves* (Houghton Mifflin, 2005), 198.
[70] Marcel Proust. *In Search of Lost Time* (Modern Library, 2003).
[71] Jonah Sachs. *Winning the Story Wars* (Harvard Business Review Press, 2012), p. 6.

weapons. "Books are like divisions or army corps: at time they must dig themselves in, hold their fire, lie low; at times they just cross bridges in the dark and noiselessly; at times, concealing their preparations to the last dribble of loose earth, they must rush into concerted offensive from the least expected quarter at the least expected moment." While it is never certain he concludes, "A shout in the mountains has been known to start an avalanche."[72] And so it was that his novel, *The Gulag Archipelago* was instrumental in the collapse of the Soviet Union. Myths combine story, explanation, and meaning in a single neat package. Movies and television dominate our realm of imaginative storytelling. However, media expert Jonah Sachs laments, "Few of our entertainers accept the responsibility of providing audiences with a genuine explanation of how the world works or offering deep meaning."[73] Storytelling is a significant cultural responsibility.

Not so abolitionist Hannah More. She understood that more than ideas, imagination moves the world. She wrote tracts, plays, and novels that sought to both instruct and delight. She was not afraid of writing for masses in a popular style. She was one of the most influential bestselling authors of her day. Some of her publications sold two million copies in less than a year.[74] She exemplified Percy Shelley's adage, "Poets are the unacknowledged legislators of the world."[75] More's biographer writes, "The battle against slavery was, in many ways, led by the poets—and other writers and artists—who expanded their country's moral imagination so it might at last see the horrors too grave for the rational mind to grasp."[76] Wilberforce would later admit that politics alone was not enough without the power of the pen to which he owed a great debt to Hannah More. Reframing demands an engagement with the imagination.

---

[72] Alexandr Solzhenitsyn. *The Oak and the Calf* (HarperCollins, 1980), p. 313, 151.
[73] Sachs, page. 63.
[74] Prior, page 125.
[75] Percy Shelly. *A Defense of Poetry*: https://www.poetryfoundation.org/articles/69388/a-defence-of-poetry/.
[76] Prior, 128.

Too often purity conferences and abstinence education organizations fail to win the frame. Meaning must precede the conviction of truthfulness. The evidence is that purity rings only delay risky sexual behavior for about six months in young adults.[77] Many abstinence presentations involve a detailed description of the twenty-five different types of sexually transmitted diseases and how condoms and other forms of contraceptives are not 100 percent reliable protection from symptoms ranging from infertility (chlamydia) to death (AIDS). Abstinence education often boils down to fear mongering. It is a veiled attempt to scare the sex out of you. "Totally worthless," my former high school students told me. "The only difference it made was that people were less hungry at lunch."[78] Katie Roiphe echoes their concerns in her book, *Last Night in Paradise: Sex and Morals at the Century's End.* "What is missing is the ideological force that pulls it all together."[79] What is missing is the priority of reframing sexuality.

Herein lies the secret to a powerful cause concept. A powerful lever must tell a concrete story that engages the imagination through a compelling picture of the telos of one's cause, and it must do so with the confidence that it is telling the truth about reality. For the final goal of cultural change is defining reality.

## Social Dynamics Rule:
*One must frame or reframe the cause concept through an engagement of the imagination. One must tell a better story.*

---

[77] Https://www.guttmacher.org/journals/psrh/2008/opposite-sex-adolescents-thoughts-about-abstinence-and-sex-and-their-sexual/.

[78] David John Seel, Jr. "Scaring the Sex Out of You," *Critique* 8, 2001, p. 4.

[79] Katie Roiphe. *Last Night in Paradise: Sex Morals at the Century's End* (Little Brown and Company, 1997), p.

# DEFINING REALITY
## The Goal of Dense Networks

*"The power of culture is the power of defining reality."*[80]
— James Davison Hunter

The challenge facing the British abolitionists was finding ways to make slavery real in the minds of the British people. The atrocities of the slave trade were largely unknown in England. The British enjoyed the products it created such as sugar and rum, but few appreciated the brutality common on sugar cane plantations in the Caribbean. Realizing the power of images, the Clapham Circle seized on a schematic representation of a slave ship, the Brookes, named for a wealthy British family of Liverpool. They printed 8,000 copies of the schematic in poster form that showed how 482 slaves could be crammed into a small ship. Typically, a quarter of the slaves died on the voyage. The stench following a slave ship was notorious. "It was said in Charleston, S.C., that when the wind was blowing off the water a certain way you could smell a slave ship before you could see it. It was a function of sickness, vomit, diarrhea, death and also the way the human body perspires in the condition of fear."[81] It was imperative that the public learn of the brutal reality of the situation. This image was later coupled with a narrative of the slave experience by the educated slave Olaudah Equiano. It was not uncommon for slaves upon being released from the holds of these ships to willingly jump overboard to their deaths. What Clapham Circle illustrated was truly a ship-born gulag. The accepted cruelty that this economy took for

---

[80] Hunter, *To Change the World,* p. 178.
[81] Mark Roth. "Slave Ships were Death Ships for Crew and Captives," *Pittsburgh Post-Gazette,* October 1, 2007: https://www.post-gazette.com/uncategorized/2007/10/01/Slave-ships-were-death-ships-for-crew-and-captives/stories/200710010247/.

granted is staggering, but much of it was outside the purview of the common citizen.[82]

It is for this reason that the focus of the culture lever must be on the telos, the expected outcome of the effort, and at the same time it must carefully frame the issue so as to address the underlying assumptions or frame. Defining reality is the highest objective of the telos and the frame. It is only when the other stakeholders in society, particularly the storytelling cultural creatives, accept this reality and then subsequently act upon it has one achieved a degree of cultural influence. Pastor Tim Keller summarized this effort: "Culture changes when a society's mind, heart, and imagination are captured by new ideas that are developed by thinkers, expounded in both scholarly and popular forms, depicted in innumerable works of art, and then lived out attractively by communities of people who are committed to them."[83] The power of culture is the power to define and embody reality for others. The cause concept must include defining reality as a major objective.

To comprehend the significance of this objective, we must first answer what do we mean when we say "culture"? What are we trying to influence? How is it formed? There are common misunderstandings about how it works, often by appealing to mass mobilization or market forces. Culture works differently from politics and business.

## The Basics of Culture[84]

Culture is basically the combination of what is accepted as taken-for-granted reality combined with what is officially articulated as reality—what is accepted as "reality" is what is accepted as

---

[82] There is more slavery and human trafficking today than in the time of Wilberforce and The Clapham Circle. Many of the shoes we wear and shirts on our backs are the fruit of inhumane sweat shops in Southeast Asia.

[83] Denis Haack. "The Transformative Power of Story," *Critique* 3, 2017, p. 8.

[84] This approach is reliant on phenomenological sociology and the sociology of knowledge often associated with Alfred Schutz and Peter Berger. This is the school of thought being reflected in this manuscript coupled with the French structuralist perspective of Pierre Bourdieu. This perspective seeks to align with school of thought reflected in the Institute for Advanced Studies in Culture at the University of Virginia.

common sense. It has both subjective symbolic features—our collective unconscious—as well as objective structural dimensions—how the assumptions of the collective unconscious are woven into the fabric of society and its institutional arrangements. Since culture is a human creation, the power of culture is the power to define reality.[85] Sociologist James Davison Hunter summarizes this point powerfully in an unpublished article, "The power of culture is not measured by the size of a cultural organization or by the quantity of its output, but by the extent to which a definition of reality is realized in the social world—taken seriously and acted upon by actors in the social world."[86] "Defining reality" then becomes the ultimate metric that matters in cultural influence. Effective cultural change requires getting agreement on a new frame through imaginatively engaged storytelling that articulates a changed telos and through that new frame provides a definition of reality that is agreed upon and acted upon by the gatekeeping culture-makers within the social world one is seeking to influence. An effective lever must include a concrete cause concept, an agreed-upon frame, a better story, with connections among the storytelling cultural creatives capable of defining reality for the wider society.

Culture is a largely invisible reality of our own creation. But it is also an objective reality that constrains the individual and eventually comes to define the individual. Peter Berger suggests that our very identity is shaped by the world we make: "Man not only produces a world, but he also produces himself. More precisely, he produces himself in a world." [87] Elsewhere he described this as a dialectical process: "Society is a human product. Society is an objective reality. Man is a social product."[88] We make

---

[85] In *The Social Construction of Reality,* Berger and Luckmann state, "the confrontation of alternative symbolic universes implies a problem of power—which of the conflicting definitions of reality will be made to stick to the society" and that "power in society includes the power to determine decisive socialization processes, and therefore, the power to produce reality." Peter Berger and Thomas Luckmann, p. 108, 119.

[86] James Davison Hunter. "Religion, Knowledge, and Power in the Modern Age," unpublished manuscript.

[87] Peter Berger. *The Sacred Canopy: Elements of a Sociological Theory of Religion* (Anchor, 1969), p. 5.

[88] Peter Berger and Thomas Luckmann. *The Social Construction of Reality* (Anchor, 1966),

culture. Culture becomes a thing. Culture in turn makes us. The three sociological terms for this three-fold process are 1) externalization, 2) objectification, and 3) internalization.

There are five things that the reader should know about culture. Knowing these premises will enable the organizational leader to better appreciate what is required in mobilizing one's dense network to define reality.

**Culture is Created**
Culture, as the sum total of our shared meanings is produced and disseminated by "reality-defining institutions." These are those national institutions that shape our public conversation and symbolic universe of meaning such as the presidency, the media, publishing houses, schools, universities, advertising agencies, and the entertainment industry. The assumption here is that culture is created rather than being implicitly embedded in, or constitutive of social arrangements. [89] Culture is more than just an epiphenomenon of economic, social or class arrangements. This means that when one is creating one's network it is essential that among its members are members of the culture-making class, those I call "*storytelling cultural creatives.*" This includes those who are in the business of symbolic creation and dissemination: academics, advertisers, media, and entertainment. These are those Richard Florida describes as the "creative class." In his 2002 book, *The Rise of the Creative Class*, he argues that regional economic advantages are no longer based on raw materials or competition for companies but the emergence of a certain kind of person. To be successful in the emerging economy, he argues one must attract and retain talented and creative people who generate innovation, develop technology-intensive industries, and as such produce and disseminate public symbolic systems of meaning or "culture." His analysis rests on the presence of three T's: talent, tolerance, and

---

p. 61.
[89] Robert Wuthnow. *Communities of Discourse* (Harvard University Press, 1989), p. 15, 16. This is the weakness of the Marxist critique of culture, which makes culture an epiphenomenon of deeper structural economics or class relationships (as seen today in many discussions on race).

technology. And while his thesis has certainly met with its critics, his insight that there are a group of people who appreciate the importance of the production of and dissemination of the stories that shape our national social imagination. If the power of story is central to cultural production, then one can assume that storytellers will be an essential role within an effective dense network. "Story," communications expert Nancy Duarte stated at the Future of Storytelling Summit in 2006, "has replaced religion as the means by which we create meaning today."[90]

## Culture is Received

French social theorist Michel Foucault states correctly that every human action is based on a "historical a priori."[91] We are more shaped by our times than we are generally capable of realizing. This is why travel and the reading of history can help us see ourselves and our times more clearly. "Travel," Mark Twain observes, "is fatal to prejudice, bigotry, and narrow-mindedness, and many of our people need it sorely on these accounts."[92] There is within every historical moment a taken-for-granted orthodoxy of assumptions, what Jonathan Haidt describes as the "opinion corridor."[93] George Orwell observed, "At any given moment there is an 'orthodoxy,' a body of ideas of which it is assumed that all right-thinking people will accept without question.... Anyone who challenges the prevailing orthodoxy finds himself silenced [*nay cancelled*] with surprising effectiveness."[94] Foucault later adds to Orwell's point, "This a priori is what, in a given period, delimits the totality of experiences in a field of knowledge, defines the mode of being of the objects that appear in that field, provides man's everyday perceptions with theoretical powers, and defines

---

[90] https://futureofstorytelling.org/. See Nancy Duarte and Patti Sanchez. *Illuminate: Ignite Change Through Speeches, Stories, Ceremonies, and Symbols* (Portfolio/Penguin, 2016).

[91] Michel Foucault. *The Archeology of Knowledge: And the Discourse on Language* (Vintage, 1982).

[92] In Phil Cousineau. *The Art of Pilgrimage.* (Conari Press, 1998), p. 12.

[93] Peter Wehner. "Jonathan Haidt Is Trying to Heal America's Divisions," *The Atlantic*, May 24, 2020: https://www.theatlantic.com/ideas/archive/2020/05/jonathan-haidt-is-trying-to-heal-america's-divisions/.

[94] George Orwell. "The Freedom of the Press," Proposed introduction to *Animal Farm*: https://www.nytimes.com/1972/10/08/archives/the-freedom-of-the-press-orwell.html/.

the conditions in which he can sustain a discourse about things that is recognized to be true."[95] Culture shapes how we see things. There is a givenness to culture as it frames not only our external conditions but the structures of our collective discourse. We see only what we expect to see. Most of our perception of reality is shaped by our unconscious mind, which has been largely shaped by our times. Therein lies the power of culture to shape our perception of reality. When a person's "received culture" no longer coincides with the surrounding mainstream culture, it will initially create cognitive dissonance, but gradually one will accommodate oneself to the surrounding culture. [96] In this context, Paul's warning, "Do not conform any longer to the pattern of this world but be transformed by the renewing of your mind" (Romans 12:2), suggests that the renewing of your mind must be a constant ongoing effort at maintaining cognitive dissonance from dominant idolatrous patterns of the surrounding culture.

## Culture is a Shared Conversation

Cultural production—that is, the reality making process—takes place within a shared community of discourse. No one acts alone and no one creates culture alone. In this sense dense networks become a "community of discourse," and this discourse is built on the tensions between the past experiences and the immediate context or, more accurately, the tensions between our taken-for-granted subconscious reality and the officially articulated public reality. [97] Police are socialized to be always wary of potential danger. Black men are socialized to be wary of police. It is for these reasons that a routine traffic stop for a Black man can easily escalate into violence. The police officer asking the Black man for

---

[95] Michel Foucault. *The Order of Things* (Random House, 1971), p. 158.
[96] This is a process that Pierre Bourdieu described as the "hysteresis of habitus." The hysteresis effect is evident when there is a disjunction between the habitus of a field and its social environment—the failure to adapt to change. In such a situation, the social group is said to be "not contemporary with themselves." See Dick Keyes, *Chameleon Christianity* (Wipf & Stock Publishers, 2003).
[97] See Wuthnow. *Communities of Discourse*, p. 18: "Accounting for cultural change requires having a clear sense of the ways in which the established producers of culture are institutionalized: of the ways in which these institutions extract resources from their environment, of their role in dramatizing and maintaining status relations, and of the status groups most likely to come to their defense."

his license and registration easily becomes the unconscious stand-in for the slave master. If the police use a certain tone, or certain words—"Boy"—the violence of the Civil War can be renewed in an instant. Culture is always a conversation between a subconscious past and a current reality.

## Culture is Disputed

Within any society, but particularly so in societies shaped by advanced modernity, culture—the shared meanings about how the world should be—is inherently contested. This contest is generally played out as a struggle over its public reality and among the creative elites that shape it.[98] Cultural meaning is usually derived from the experiences or choices of private individuals but is mediated through "reality-defining" institutions and those cultural elites—storytelling cultural creatives—who are in a position to engage in these symbolic battles. *Cultural conflict is intrinsically undemocratic. It is a discourse of elites and among elites.* And if we are interested in shaping these conversations, then we need to have access to these conversations. Recent cultural conflicts are not simply economic (between the rich and the poor) or racial (between white people and people of color), but between competing moral visions about the nature of reality. There are four types of culture-makers: those who engage in the production, distribution, application, or administration of cultural symbols of meaning. These culture-makers are foundationally defined not by the content of their ideology—whether religious, political, economic, or moral, left or right—but rather by their function. The distinguishing factor of these elites is their *access to reality-defining organizations* (radio airwaves, cable news, university classrooms, corporate markets, and the like) and their *monopoly over specialized knowledge*. It is not the masses that matter in this public reality-defining function, but these elites and the dense networks in which they participate. Culture then is that arena where competing communities of discourse or dense networks compete for resources, gain access to reality-defining

---

[98] This is what is playing out in the "woke" and "cancel culture" public debate on cable news.

55

organizations, and articulate in a compelling manner their take on reality. Peter Berger states this point bluntly, "The fundamental coerciveness of society lies not in its machineries of social control, but in its power to constitute and impose itself as reality."[99] Culture-shaping ideas are always mediated through dense networks, which are themselves controlled by gatekeepers who have the prerequisite cultural, social, economic, and symbolic capital to have access to these networks. Access to these reality-defining national public institutions is critical for cultural change.

## Culture is Both Strategic and Tactical

Strategy is the art of maneuvering resources prior to an engagement, whereas tactics is the art of maneuver after one is fully engaged. Strategy and tactics are important because there are no truces or timeouts in the process of cultural influence. As we will examine in the next chapter, when the gay movement leadership that met in Warrenton, Virginia in 1988 was doing so in the midst of an AIDS crisis largely ignored by the Reagan administration that was spawning a homophobic backlash in the mainstream public. The strategic decisions made at this gathering were in the midst of a messy, costly, and uncertain social context.

Likewise this book is an exercise in strategy, focusing on the requirement, characteristics, and dynamics of dense networks for leveraging cultural influence. Its rules can be ignored, used badly for partisan political or religiously tribal purposes, or used for constructive spiritual and civic purposes. One should from this book ideally be able to assess the strengths and weaknesses of one's relational network, make the appropriate changes, and in time achieve more effective cultural leverage for the sake of the common good.

The purpose of dense networks is not to better empower evangelical culture warriors. It is not to deny the reality of the American church's cultural exile status. But dense networks can be

---

[99] Peter Berger. *The Sacred Canopy: Elements of a Sociological Theory of Religion* (Anchor Books, 1990), p. 12.

aimed to wisely empower shalom within the spheres of social influence that one is directed to by calling, whether personal or institutional. It is the most effective means of achieving faithful presence. Most of the church's efforts at cultural engagement are ineffectual or worse, counterproductive. It is time to once again learn from those who have been able to make a substantial cultural difference by aligning ourselves to the ontological dynamics of or sociological rules of dense networks. If dense networks are the way social reality works, then we had better align ourselves with their inherent social dynamics and rules. This starts by acknowledging that we are ultimately in the reality-defining business.

## Social Dynamics Rule:

*The power of culture is the power to define reality and to have that definition acted on by reality-defining storytelling cultural creatives.*

# THE LOVE THAT DARES NOT SPEAK ITS NAME

## The Campaign for Equal Rights

*"Equality means more than passing laws. The struggle is
really won in the hearts and minds of the community,
where it really counts."*[100]
— Barbara Gittings

Many Americans are unfamiliar with Black history. To combat
this ignorance, since 1976 every U.S. president has officially
designated the month of February as Black History Month.
However, Americans are even more ignorant of the history of the
gay rights movement. This is unfortunate because the cultural
acceptance of gay rights is one of the most impressive recent
cultural transformations and example of dense networks in social
change, which culminated in the Supreme Court acceptance of
same-sex marriage in 2015 and additional protection from
employment discrimination in 2020. Even if one disagrees with
these efforts, one can appreciate and learn from what it took to
accomplish this social change. At the heart of this story is the
power of dense networks. This is a remarkable cultural
achievement.[101]

For many years, the gay community was closeted and hidden from
public view. Keeping it this way was what the straight society
preferred. As Marshall Kirk and Hunter Madsen put it, "We think
gays must never underestimate straight society's desire and

---

[100] Summer Kurtz. "How Barbara Gittings Changed the World," *Travel Pride*, October 9, 2017:
https://medium.com/travelpride/lgbt-history-month-how-barbara-gittings-changed-the-world-
e943928d37d3/.
[101] While I am not a member of this community, I am an aggressive ally. As a social scientist, I
am awed by what they have accomplished against such widespread cultural and religious
stigma in such a short period of time.

capacity not to see them, to make them invisible, even during the AIDS crisis."[102] The gay equality movement began with the Stonewall riots in New York City in June 1969. For the next decade, gay equality made enormous public progress.

Considering the widespread moral offense associated with the movement, it achieved significant gains in the 1970s. In 1970, gay pride and protest marches were held in Chicago, Los Angeles, New York City, and San Francisco around the first anniversary of The Stonewall Riot. The American Psychiatric Association removed homosexuality from its list of psychiatric disorders, some cities and states overturned laws criminalizing homosexuality, there was the first gay television movie (*That Certain Summer*, 1972), the first openly gay official in the history of California was elected to the San Francisco Board of Supervisors (Harvey Milk, 1977), and the Briggs Initiative (Proposition 6) was defeated in California (1978). The failed Briggs Initiative sought to ban gays and lesbians from working in California's public schools. These successes were quickly challenged.

The rapid cultural and increasingly public acceptance of gay equality led to a widespread cultural backlash in the late 1970s. Singer Anita Bryant led a successful drive in 1977 to repeal a gay-rights ordinance in Dade County, Florida. Harvey Milk was assassinated in November of 1978. In July 3, 1981, *The New York Times* ran a forbidding headline foreshadowing what was to come: "Rare Cancer Seen in 41 Homosexuals."[103] The AIDS epidemic had begun.

It became an incurable "gay cancer," which further expanded the cultural stigma and fear associated with homosexuals. Religious leaders falsely and harshly claimed that it was God's judgment on their immoral lifestyle. The fear associated with AIDS in the early 1980s was palpable. At this time, AIDS was 100% fatal, with a mortality velocity from diagnosis to death being four months, and

---

[102] Marshall Kirk and Hunter Madsen. *After the Ball: How America Will Conquer Its Fear & Hatred of Gays in the 90's* (Plume, 1990), p. 18.
[103] Https://www.nytimes.com/1981/07/03/us/rare-cancer-seen-in-41-homosexuals.html/.

even more alarming, no one knew how the disease was contracted. The 2013 film *The Dallas Buyers Club* and the 2018 documentary about the first AIDS ward, *5B*, captures the AIDS stigma of the 1980s accurately. It is important not to forget about the ravages and fear of AIDS.

I know this because I lived it personally. A close family member died in our home of AIDS in 1990. He was gay and had been living in the Castro district of San Francisco. At the time we turned our home into an AIDS ward, my children were ages 10 and 12. We had to notify the neighboring families of my children's friends of his presence in our home. We lived the 1993 film *Philadelphia*. AIDS is a terrible way to die. But the fear and stigma associated with the illness only compounded the loneliness and the lack of physical contact faced by the brave patients who contracted the disease.

The eight years of the Reagan administration were a disaster for the gay equality movement. Reagan's first mention of AIDS was in 1987, six years after the start of the pandemic. Many LGBTQ+ people felt abandoned by their country. The gay equality progress of the 1970s gave way to the escalating tragedy of the 1980s. The past advances in acceptance gave way to scapegoating denunciations. This history is refreshed as a way of highlighting the enormous accomplishments achieved by LGBTQ+ activists since then. Few can appreciate the amount of fear and stigma that then surrounded the public perception of the gay community. Marshall Kirk and Hunter Madsen frankly state in their national bestseller, "The only thing worse than being a 'Mary'" in this society is being a Typhoid Mary. Here, alas, homosexuality itself became a telltale sign of the century's most dreaded disease."[104] Stigma and fear were the operative realities. It was at this cultural low point that the LGBTQ+ movement turned to the power of dense networks. As they say, the rest is history. But it is particularly important to appreciate the social barriers this movement overcame.

---

[104] Marshall Kirk and Hunter Madsen, p. 25.

## The War Conference

Over the weekend of February 26, 1988, 150 LGBTQ+ equality leaders met at Airlie House in Warrenton, Virginia, 50 miles west of Washington, D.C. The gathering was billed as a "War Conference" "to draft strategies for pushing effective AIDS legislation and to combat what their leaders say is growing homophobia in America."[105] Six months earlier, the home of two hemophiliac children with AIDS are firebombed in Arcadia, Florida, after parents protested letting the two children attend their public school. It was not hyperbole to call this a "war conference."

From this gathering emerged a dense network and a remarkable strategy. In the "Final Statement of the War Conference," they state, "We need to establish a national emergency response network that will link all organizations—local, state, and national—to provide the means for quickly generating the calls, telegrams, letters, and mailgrams we need to pressure elected officials. We must use our existing organizations and community groups, with the technical assistance of groups like ACTUP to help build the system we need. In addition to providing an emergent response in times of crisis, the system can be used to communicate on routine matters." [106] There were certainly tensions and differences of opinions expressed at the conference between the assimilationist groups and their radical counterparts.

Some wanted to move immediately to politics to address pressing concerns about violence towards LGBTQ+ individuals, lack of child custody laws, and pervasive workplace discrimination. The palpable outrage of LGBTQ+ activists was justifiable. And while some of these legal efforts moved forward, the overarching sentiment and direction following the conference was to address the underlying consciousness of "straight" America. It was a restrained agenda.

---

[105] "Gay Rights Leaders Gather in Virginia," *United Press International*, February 27, 1988.
[106] "Final Statement of The War Conference":
https://rmc.library.cornell.edu/HRC/exhibition/stage/REX023_164.pdf/.

They adopted a distinctly cultural strategy, one articulated in an article written by Marshall Kirk and Erastes Pill (the pen name of Hunter Madsen) published two months earlier in *Guide Magazine*, "The Overhauling of Straight America." [107] They argued that LGBTQ+ people must portray themselves in a positive way to "straight" America, to make it "no big deal." They sought to reframe the debate over LGBTQ+ equality from sex to human rights, from abnormal to normal, from rare to common, and from weird to mainstream. It was a modest agenda that got behind the overt cultural controversies to address underlying attitudes with a clear telos. "We are seeking public desensitization and nothing more. We do not need and cannot expect a full 'appreciation' or 'understanding' of homosexuality from the average American. You can forget about trying to persuade the masses that LGBTQ+ equality is a good thing. But if only you can get them to think that it is just another thing, with a shrug of their shoulders, then your battle for legal and social rights is virtually won," they argued.[108] The effort was made to normalize the idea of homosexual behavior in effect to make it pass within "straight" America. It was assumed that LGBTQ+ people needed to be made to look less flamboyant, less scary: "they should be indistinguishable from the straights we would like to reach." The goal was to move from Liberace to Anderson Cooper. They argue, "If gays are presented as a strong and prideful tribe promoting a rigidly nonconformist and deviant lifestyle, they are more likely to be seen as a public menace that justifies resistance and oppression."[109] It was the modesty of this proposal that enabled the LGBTQ+ community to be viewed by the wider straight public eventually as victims. They made a point of enlisting the national storytelling cultural creatives: "So far, gay Hollywood has provided our best covert weapon in the battle to desensitize the mainstream."[110] The NBC television sitcom, "Will & Grace," began airing on September 21, 1998. President Joe Biden

---

[107] Http://library.gayhomeland.org/0018/EN/EN_Overhauling_Straight.htm/.
[108] Ibid.
[109] Ibid.

[110] Marshall K. Kirk and Hunter Madsen. "Waging Peace: A Gay Battle Plan to Persuade Straight America," *Christopher Street,* 1985.

commented that the show, "probably did more to educate the American public," on LGBTQ+ issues, "than almost anything anybody has ever done so far."[111] It influenced his own change of heart on the issue.

The history and success of the LGBTQ+ equality movement is of course much more complicated and detailed than what I have outlined here.[112] Sometimes added details only serve to obscure the underlying outline of the gay rights activists' success: 1) they established a dense network in the spirit of national institutional collaboration, 2) addressed the underlying framing of the issue they were addressing, 3) focused on culture before politics, and 4) garnered the support of storytelling cultural creatives and the reality-defining institutions in which they worked.

Faith-based critics of the LGBTQ+ equality agenda have flagged this conference and this paper as significant, one calling it, "an actual PR blueprint for efforts to gain acceptance of homosexual behavior over the past 30 years."[113] But sadly few have stopped to fully appreciate what they accomplished and how. There is much to be learned from their example. The story here is one of a lever, a fulcrum, and a world.

---

[111] David Eldridge. "Biden 'comfortable' with Gay Marriage. cites 'Will & Grace.'" *The Washington Times*, Sunday, May 6, 2012.
[112] For a thorough history of gay rights one should read Lillian Faderman's *The Gay Revolution: The Story of the Struggle* (Simon & Schuster, 2016). For a companion history of the AIDS pandemic, Ronald Bayer and Gerald Oppenheimer's *AIDS Doctors: Voices from the Epidemic* (Oxford, 2002). Howard Markel. "Journals of the Plague Years: Documenting the History of the AIDS Epidemic in the United States," *American Journal of Public Health*, Vol. 91, July 1, 2001.
[113] Joe Carter. "The Most Influential Essay You've Never Heard Of," *The Christian Post*, April 7, 2014.

# THE FULCRUM

# TWO TYPES OF DENSE NETWORKS
## Mentors and Schools

*"Great ideas are produced by humans who are linked to one another.*
*The construction of philosophical ideas is thus embedded in the social*
*structure of the intellectual world."*[114]
— Ilan Talmud

The fulcrum represents the dense network itself. It is thus a metaphor for a certain kind of grouping of people. It is to this aspect of our overarching picture that we now turn.

The relational nature of dense networks, and the proliferation of them throughout history, can be seen in two types: professional mentorship (or master-apprentice chains) and schools of thought. The former is more common, the latter more consequential. The latter is also more difficult to sustain because of its tendency toward abstraction. There are important lessons to be learned from both.

### Master-Apprentice Chains
Mentorship and discipleship have too often been viewed in individualistic terms. It is more useful to see them as emerging dense networks. Certain disciplines have strict rules of apprenticeship, with a formalized hierarchy of master-student relationships. In the past these were more common and had greater influence over the course of one's career. With an appreciation for carrying on the traits of the master, the

---

[114] Ilan Talmud. "Review of Randall Collins: *The Sociology of Philosophies: A Global Theory of Intellectual Change*," *European Sociological Review*, Vol. 15, No. 3 (Sep., 1999), pp. 342-345.

apprentice's work would be expected to carry on the mark of the master. My father was a surgeon who studied at Tulane Medical School under the legendary surgeon and medical researcher Alton Ochsner. He was proud to describe himself as one of the "Oschner boys." And so it is within the academy, and historically in guilds, that there are intergenerational network linkages established by apprenticeship programs and mentoring relationships. When seminary education was more based on the apprenticeship to a noted preacher or theologian, this was also common in the church. It is still common in graduate school education. Doctoral advisors historically have a lasting professional influence on the academic approach and professional productivity of their graduate students. This is why they are often mentioned on one's vita. Some professions have structurally integrated these dynamics into their professional legitimation process as formal master-pupil chains. Here there is a tacit responsibility of the apprentice to follow in the footsteps of the master. It is not uncommon for institutes to be formed around these masters to carry on these relational legacies and the techniques and values they embrace, such as in the Ochsner Medical Center.

The master-pupil network model isn't limited only to academia. Within the National Football League there are significant coaching networks based both on apprenticeship and close relational ties. In many cases the hiring decisions of NFL coaches is weighted by one's network associations. The following coaches have the most protégés: Chuck Noll (35), Don Shula (39), Mark Levy (36), Dan Reeves (66), Bill Belichick (45), Joe Gibbs (41), Bill Parcells (47), and Mike Holmgren (41).[115] Bill Belichick and Andy Reid have a huge contemporary influence within the NFL coaching network.

However, as the structures of professions have changed and individual entrepreneurship has been increasingly celebrated, the continuity and force of these master-pupil networks have

---

[115] Andrew Fast and David Jensen. "The NFL Coaching Network: Analysis of the Social Network Among Professional Football Coaches," *American Association for Artificial Intelligence*, January 2006.

weakened. But in the past, this was the most common way that dense networks were formed. University of Pennsylvania sociologist Randall Collins observes, "The history of philosophy is to a considerable extent the history of groups. Nothing abstract is meant here—nothing, but groups of friends, discussion partners, close-knit circles that often have the characteristics of social movements."[116] One example is the Inklings, the informal literary discussion group that included C.S. Lewis and J.R.R. Tolkien that met at the back of the Eagle and the Child pub in Oxford for nearly two decades between the early 1930s and the late 1940s.[117]

It remains true that all thoughtful leaders have an intellectual pedigree; those whose writing, thought, and mentorship have had a lasting personal impact. I certainly have mine, and thoughtful readers can generally trace the echoes of their influence (C.S. Lewis, Francis Schaeffer, Dallas Willard, Charles Taylor, and my father, David Seel). But what is generally missing in an intellectual pedigree is a sense of formal obligation, tight relational bond, or shared mission that is characteristic of an effective dense network. Dense networks require both a high degree of sociability and solidarity: relational commitment and missional solidarity. This will be explained more fully in the next chapter. The effectiveness of master-pupil chains is their high relational sociability even more than their missional solidarity. The sociability bond is where master-pupil chains gain their force and leverage.

### Schools of Thought

Less common, but far more effective for long-term social influence are dense networks that are associated with developing a particular "school of thought." These are networks that highlight a high degree of missional solidarity and/or commitment to a specific intellectual approach or belief system. Sociologist Randall Collins found that the history of philosophy is really a history of small groups of competing intellectual dense networks. He writes,

---

[116] Randall Collins. *The Sociology of Philosophies: A Global Theory of Intellectual Change* (Harvard University Press, 1998), p. 3.
[117] Humphrey Carpenter. *The Inklings: C.S. Lewis, J.R.R. Tolkien, Charles Williams and their Friends*, (Harper Collins, 1979).

"Intellectuals make their breakthroughs, changing the course of the flow of ideas, because of what they do with the cultural capital and emotional energy flowing down to them from their own pasts, restructured by the networks of tensions among their contemporaries." [118] In his mammoth overview of intellectual history, Collins found that the total number of philosophers who are significant in world history is limited to approximately 135, because it is the groups or schools of thought that matters, not the individuals. He concludes, "It is the network which write[s] the plot of this story; and the structure of the network competition over the attention space, which determines creativity, is focused so that the famous ideas become formulated through the mouths and pens of few individuals. To say that the community of creative intellectuals is small is really to say that the networks are focused at a few peaks."[119]

At any given moment of history within a particular field of discourse there are never more than six players, or "*the Big Six*." It is the competitive discourse between these three- to- six players that writes the history of philosophy. These communities of discourse certainly have some relational connectivity, but even more they share a common point of view or school of thought. It is the clarity of this point of view or school of thought that gives the network its oppositional force with the field of discourse. Without clarity, there is less opposition. It is the drama of opposition between schools of thought that sets these networks apart from one another. The main point here is that dense networks can be formed from either a relational dynamic or a shared point of view. To this end, they reflect the needed balance of sociability and solidarity, to which we now turn. When a network is able to combine these two powerful dynamics together, sociability and solidarity—strong relationships and shared perspective, it has a particular advantage or leverage within their field of influence.

---

[118] Collins, p. 60.

[119] Ibid. 78.

# Social Dynamics Rule:

*Dense networks are either formed around master-apprentice relationships or a shared school of thought. Both have their strengths and weaknesses.*

# SOCIABILITY AND SOLIDARITY
## Psychological Dynamics of Dense Networks

*"Social networks are the structures that human beings
naturally form, beginning with knowledge
itself and the various forms of representation
we use to communicate it."[120]*
— Niall Ferguson

In our picture, the fulcrum is the network itself. They are typically formed in one of two ways—around a shared set of relationships or a shared set of ideas. Balancing these factors is critical for a successful dense network.

We will not pay much attention as to how one attracts a network. More important than how they form is how they function. The collective dynamics of a particular dense network serves as its culture, comprised of its widely shared values, symbols, behaviors, and assumptions. More colloquially we might say that our culture is, "how we get things done around here." It comes down to a common way of thinking, which drives a common way of acting, reflecting a shared definition of reality. But to assess the strengths and weaknesses of a dense network's culture, we need to discuss factors that are more quantitative and measurable, less amorphous and intuitive.

First, a dense network is more than a collection of separate individuals. It becomes a separate thing in itself, what Emile Durkheim calls a "social fact."[121] A dense network is designated as a social fact when its group behavior is distinct from any one's individual behavior. When a dense network becomes a social fact,

---

[120] Niall Ferguson. *The Square and the Tower: Networks and Power, from the Freemasons to Facebook* (Penguin Press, 2018), p. 17.
[121] Emile Durkheim. *The Rules of Sociological Method* (Free Press, 2014), p. 20.

it operates much like a group of starlings, called a *"murmuration,"* or a school of fish.

George F. Young and his colleagues investigated starlings' "remarkable ability to maintain cohesion as a group in highly uncertain environments and with limited, noisy information."[122] Young knew that starlings pay attention to a fixed number of their neighbors in the flock, regardless of flock density. His discovery was that the number was seven. When the birds interact with six or seven neighbors, one gets the optimized balance between group cohesiveness and individual effort.[123] People in social groups operate in a similar manner. When a dense network develops its own collaborative identity that reflects both individual effort and collective coordination, we can say that the dense network has entered "the zone"—balancing sociality and solidarity in maximum effectiveness. Balance is the goal.

There are two main variables that factor into creating this experience of maximum collective coordination: sociability or relational attachment and solidarity or missional attachment. No dense network or organization is going to be successful without carefully attending to its internal culture and the balance between sociability and solidarity. These are variables originally derived from the French social philosopher Émile Durkheim.[124]

### Network Sociability
Sociability is a measure of relational friendliness between the members of a community. It has to do with a set of mutual expectations or the hidden social bond between them. Here,

---

[122] George F. Young, Luca Scardovi, Andrea Cavagna, Irene Giardina, and Naomi E. Leonard. "Starling Flock
Networks Manage Uncertainty in Consensus at Low Cost." *Journal of Public Library of Science-Computational
Biology*, January 31, 2013.
[123] Anna Azvolinsky. "Birds of a Feather... Track Seven Neighbors to Flock Together," Princeton University:
https://www.princeton.edu/news/2013/02/07/birds-feather-track-seven-neighbors-flock-together?section=topstories/.
[124] Emile Durkheim. *The Division of Labor in Society* (Free Press, 2014). This chapter expands on the work of Rob Goffee and Gareth Jones, *The Character of a Corporation* (Harvard Business Press, 1998).

relationships are king. In mathematical discussions of networks, theorists speak of "*network density*." The density of a given social network is found by dividing the number of all existing actual links between the actors by the number of potential links within the same set of actors. The higher the resulting number, the denser a network is.

For example, the actual connections between people at a family reunion are generally high. In contrast, the actual connections between people on a bus—the number of people who actually know each other—is likely to be quite low. Network density has to do with the degree of *actual connections* within a network. This is a meaningful distinction to keep in mind particularly when one is talking about Facebook "friends." A large network of Facebook friends could quite easily have a low network density—depending on how the Facebook network was compiled. Where there is a high degree of sociability, community values prevail, teamwork is common, and free exchange of information is fostered because there is a high level of trust.

There are, however, downsides to high sociability, namely that the boundaries between personal and public are often blurred. Moreover, friendships can tend to allow for poor performance to be tolerated. The common experience of small towns becomes prevalent, as in everyone's business is everyone's business. This is mentioned because all of the positives of sociability can mask the dangers of psychological enmeshment and poor boundary maintenance. In this case, dysfunctional high sociability can tend to weaken solidarity, when maintaining a relationship, saving face, or avoiding conflict becomes an excuse for poor performance or commitment to mission.

In the composition of a dense network's sociability, relational depth also needs to be balanced by relational breadth. If a network becomes too relationally ingrown, it weakens its potential scope of influence. In effect an inwardly oriented clique forms. In network science, relational breadth is enhanced by the "*power of weak ties*"—the power of mere acquaintances. "When it comes to finding a job, getting news, launching a restaurant, or spreading the latest fad, our weak social ties are more important than our cherished strong friendships."[125] Weak ties or acquaintances serve as bridges to new networks even more than close friends. To get new information or foster innovation, one must activate weak ties. This suggests that network density must be balanced with weak ties.

While it is not a perfect analogy, something of this combination of strong and weak ties is seen even among Jesus' disciples. Peter and Andrew were brothers and shared the same occupation, fishing. The same is true of James and John. Collectively, these four served as the inner circle, with Peter, James, and John as the core of that inner circle. These three were the ones with Jesus at the healing of Jarius' daughter (Mark 5:22-48) and were taken with Jesus to the mount of Transfiguration (Matthew 17:1-8). Andrew was formerly a follower of John the Baptist. Together, these four had blood and occupational ties as fishermen that suggests a strong social linkage. Philip and Nathanael were also close friends. Matthew and James the Lesser were both brothers. This leaves four who were in the outer ring of the apostles: Thomas, Jude Thaddeus, Simon, and Judas Iscariot. Two-thirds have high social density and a third have less. It's mere speculation to suggest that Jesus was intuitively operating on the basis of network science, but it does suggest that a quarter to third of the composition of one's dense network needs to be composed of those with weak ties compared to the inner circle of the dense network. If, for example, one is building a dense network based primarily on recent Ivy League graduates (Harvard, Princeton, Yale), in order to avoid an insularity of perspective and connections one should also select a quarter to a third from less prestigious colleges and universities. One may want to balance the degree of privilege and the narrow perspective it affords in one's network. The point here is that sociability not only has to be balanced with solidarity but the character of the social relations

---

[125] Barabási, p. 42.

73

themselves needs to be balanced between strong and weak ties. It is also true that the loss of a person with a weak tie is more damaging to the network than the loss of a person with a strong tie. This is because the person with the weak tie will take with them an entire ancillary network for which they were potentially the only connection.

If the dense network is all weak ties, one will have low density and weak sociability. If it is all strong ties, one will have high density and insulated sociability, which will impact the breadth of the network's potential influence and openness to innovation. The Clapham Circle benefited greatly from those who did not live around the Clapham Common, nor shared common blood or matrimonial ties, particularly evidenced in Hannah More, the playwright who brought in an entirely new network of literary relationships outside of politics to the movement both from Bristol and London.[126]

Research has also shown that dense networks are very difficult to manage when over 150 members. The corporate anthropologist Robin Dunbar found that 150 persons is the measurement of the "cognitive limit to the number of individuals with whom any one person can maintain stable relationships."[127] There is wisdom in breaking networks into more manageable pods of 150 individuals. It is not particularly surprising to discover that the average church size in America is in the 75-to-184-person range.[128]

## Network Solidarity
In contrast to sociability is solidarity, which is defined as the members' level of commitment to the mission or cause concept of the dense network. Solidaristic relationships are based on common tasks, mutual interests, and shared goals. Here it does not matter whether you like your co-member, just whether you are

---

[126] Karen Swallow Prior. *Fierce Convictions.*
[127] Peter Cook: https://petercook.com/blog/the-magic-of-150/. Robin Dunbar. *How Many Friends Does One Person*
*Need? Dunbar's Number and Other Evolutionary Quirks* (Faber & Faber, 2010).
[128] Https://prodigalthought.net/2011/01/26/the-average-church-size-in-america/.

able to get the job done. Here, the mission is king. Police departments are an example of high solidarity networks. Members might dislike each other personally, but you would never know it when at work. Marketing guru Harry Beckwith reminds us that there is a fallacy to leadership. He writes, "Few Americans yearn to be managed; most talented people despise the very idea. You do not manage people. You create a business they care so much about that they don't require management; create goals so compelling that your employees manage themselves to achieve them."[129] Solidarity is about having a compelling purpose.

When solidarity is high at the expense of sociability, the network will have a piercing focus and a kind of ruthlessness. Outside investors like high solidarity organizations because of their efficiency and because they don't have to work there. Solidarity, too, has a dark side. High solidarity cultures can be brutal where compassion to the individual is abandoned in favor of a do-or-die attitude. Think Mafia.

When an organization has been without a leader for some time, it is not uncommon for different departments to develop their own agendas. This is also a challenge in the increasingly common virtual organizations that are often networks of divergent consulting agendas. In these cases, solidarity to mission will erode.

There are some organizations that are weak in both sociability and solidarity making them particularly difficult to manage. This is the character of the large modern university.[130]

For a dense network to get in the zone—to work at peak capacity—these two variables of sociability and solidarity need to get in balance and in focus. They are not mutually exclusive. But it doesn't happen easily or automatically. Maintaining balance is

---

[129] Harry Beckwith. *The Invisible Touch: The Four Keys to Modern Marketing* (Warner Books, 2000), p. 38.
[130] Alasdair MacIntyre. "The End of Education: The Fragmentation of the American University," *Commonweal*, 2006: https://metanexus.net/end-education-fragmentation-american-university/.

only possible with the self-conscious input from collaborative leadership. Effective dense networks do not happen by accident. We will speak about the kind of leadership needed in a subsequent chapter.

## Network Assessment
An organizational leader must begin by assessing the current state of one's organizational network. One needs to ask questions both about the network's sociability and solidarity.

*Sociability*
1. To what degree are the relationships in the network more than mere acquaintances?
2. Do the members have a sense of personal or professional obligation to one another?
3. Are the members doing things together or involved in shared projects?
4. What percentage of the network is comprised of weak ties?
5. What is the area of sociability most needing attention—density or composition—to get the network in the zone?

*Solidarity*
1. Do the members share a defined mission that they can articulate?
2. Do they sense a responsibility of being on a defined "team"?
3. To what extent is the cause concept recognized and formally defined?
4. What is the area of solidarity most needing attention to get the network in the zone?

## Network Types
The twofold emphasis on network sociability and solidarity creates a graph of four potential types of networks: fragmented,

mercenary, networked, and communal. To determine your network's culture, ask these four test questions:

1. What is my use of physical space?
2. What is the nature of the organization's communication?
3. What is the balance of use of time for life and work?
4. What is a member's sense of identity?
5. How does the organization handle success or failure?

These are the concrete ways that sociability and solidarity are expressed within an organization.

From this determination, one will find four types of culture: fragmented (low sociability and low solidarity), mercenary (low sociability and high solidarity), networked (high sociability and low solidarity), and communal (high sociability and high solidarity).[131]

---

[131] Goffee and Jones, p. 21.

# Two Dimensions, Four Cultures

| | | |
|---|---|---|
| high | Networked | Communal |
| | Fragmented | Mercenary |
| low | low      Solidarity      high | |

(Sociability on vertical axis; Solidarity on horizontal axis)

When this matrix is applied to dense networks, one should always be always seeking to create the communal culture. This is also the hardest to create and maintain. We will focus our attention here on the communal culture that combines the friendship process-orientation from the networked culture and the results-orientation from the mercenary. Goffee and Jones explain that, "communal cultures involve high levels of intimacy, respect, and kindness among their members—that's the sociability part—but their high solidarity also requires members to put the organization's goals first, even when it means shutting down debate or eliminating poor performance." [132] The rules of survival in a communal network are:

---

[132] Ibid. 37.

78

1. Join the family.
2. Love the cause.
3. Live the credo.
4. Follow the leader.
5. Fight the good fight.

In a communal network, one's identity gets wrapped up in the cause, and it is not uncommon for the lines between one's public and personal life get blurred. One can see this both in the Clapham Circle as well as the gay rights movement where the identity of the members and the cause run together.

The role of leadership is critical in a communal dense network. A charismatic collaborative leader serves as a high-profile model for the behaviors of both sociability and solidarity and is beneficial for an effective dense network. We see this illustrated in Harvey Milk, who led the gay rights movement in the Castro District in San Francisco prior to his untimely death. It is said of such leaders that they trail myths behind them. Milk certainly fits this assessment as depicted in the 2008 film that bears his name.

The culture of an organization or dense network will naturally devolve toward a fragmented state unless management input is added to the equation and maintained. The Clapham Circle devolved quickly upon the abolition of slavery and Wilberforce's death in 1833.

It should be clear that effective dense networks do not normally emerge on their own. For there are particular characteristics and composition that make them effective. As we will see, when these cultural and structural factors of the network are then empowered by the members' intrinsic motivations, its synergy and effectiveness are further compounded. When this happens, dense networks become movements.

# Social Dynamics Rule:

*Dense networks must balance the inevitable
tensions between sociability and solidarity.*

# EMPOWERING MOTIVATIONS

*"Ideas don't succeed in history because of their inherent truthfulness, but rather because of their connection to very powerful institutions and interests."*[133]
— Peter Berger

An essential role of the collaborative leadership in a dense network is balancing the competing demands of sociability and solidarity among the members of the network. However, there is an additional structural step that truly enables a dense network to enter the zone: enabling the members of the dense network to align their individual motivations to the mission of the network. When this happens, the catalytic force on the lever is shared among all the members of the network. Every member becomes an effective player. Encouraging each member's personal ownership and stake in the cause concept is key to create this effectiveness.

### Turning an Ideas into a Movement
When I was working as the Director of Cultural Engagement at the John Templeton Foundation, I had the opportunity to attend various national leadership ideas conferences such as the Aspen Ideas Festival, The Nantucket Project, Milken Global Summit, and Pop Tech.

I learned about turning ideas into a movement at a workshop at Pop Tech. Pop Tech was founded by John Sculli after he left Apple. The Pop Tech conference serves as the annual gathering of a robust community of remarkable scientists, humanitarians, technologists, designers, artists, innovators, corporate and

---

[133] Quoted in James Davison Hunter, "To Change the World," Unpublished manuscript, 2002, p. 4.

governmental leaders, academics, and those who defy tidy categorization. The purpose of the event is to explore, inspire, instigate and discover a shared potential that extends well beyond the reach of individual aspiration. The event is designed to push the limits of possibility—to create new territory for collaborative exploration. At PopTech you'll find fewer celebrities than at TED and Aspen and much less backslapping. Instead, you'll meet 600 extraordinary, ordinary people stranded together in Camden, Maine, who have no alternative but to talk to each other and make connections.

In light of my cultural engagement portfolio at Templeton, I was intrigued by an afternoon breakout session that promised to teach one how to turn an idea into a movement. Through a driving rainstorm, I made my way to a converted restaurant where the session was being held. I was heartened to see the famed author Parker Palmer also in attendance. The session was being hosted by a Portland-based consulting firm, Context Partners, whose CEO has the memorable name Charlie Brown. There was some wonderful locally prepared food available for the participants which we tasted as things settled. As a group, we were then presented a real business problem facing a local restauranteur in the Camden area whose owner was present. We were tasked with solving this business problem, but first we had to choose a group of people who shared our dominant personal motivations. On a white board were listed the six groups we could choose to join:

1. Curator
2. Innovator
3. Builder
4. Storyteller
5. Connector, and
6. Sharer.

A brief description of each group was given, and we then went to the area assigned to one of the six groups. I have often described my strength professionally as, "putting legs on a vision." So, I went to the "builders" group. Parker Palmer, I suspect, went to the storytellers' group. For about thirty minutes, we collectively brainstormed on solutions to the problem presented from the perspective of builders.

Afterwards, all six groups came back together, and all of the insights were gathered on a large wall in a collaborative discussion with the owner. This portion went on for another forty-five minutes. What emerged on that wall was truly amazing. At first, it was a room filled with highly capable and accomplished people—attendees of Pop Tech—but what emerged was more than just good idea; it was real collective enthusiasm for the solutions being presented.

In the closing fifteen minutes, Pop Tech explained what we had just experienced: a tactile encounter with food beautifully displayed from the restaurant we were discussing; a presentation of a rational business problem; the opportunity to align our personal motivations and gifting around that problem; and the opportunity to be heard collectively, with Context Partners merely facilitating and curating the discussion.

Rather than teach their thesis, we experienced it: successful networks gain traction when people's individual motivations are aligned with the shared network goal. Context Partners has found from repeated consulting experience that effective dense networks need these six kinds of members. These six have been reinforced in my own work with clients. My guess is that your dense network is missing more than half of these, nor have you empowered your members to align their motivations in service to the shared effort at cultural leverage. Courtney O'Brien, a senior design strategist at Context Partners, reminds us, "Platforms alone don't cultivate a community or build movements. Relationships do…. This work has taught the importance of investing in your relational strategy first: what do you aim to achieve, who do you need with you to achieve it, what do they need from one another to get there? Only then is it appropriate to ask, how can technology deliver what our community needs at scale?"[134]

The aspirational goal of a dense network—in terms of our overarching picture—is powerfully aligning the lever to the fulcrum to a defined world. Too often overlooked in this process is empowering members in the network to act according to their intrinsic motivations. When people are able to align their own psychological motivations around a shared cause and are empowered to use them in service to the cause, participation in the dense network becomes aligned to their own identity in a powerful way. I saw it happen in a pop-up network of strangers at Pop Tech.

This process demands three steps: alignment, choice, and listening. First, recognize that when people get aligned with their own psychological motivations, they are empowered. People have differing strengths and motivations. Too often leaders gather around themselves people who are just like them and this is a fatal weakness. Needed is a unified diversity.

Second, people need to be able to choose their own group. The empowering must begin at the beginning. Ownership of the process must be the starting point.

Third, people need to be heard and have their insights acted upon. This cannot be theoretical exercise, but one in which the solutions offered are solutions that are acted upon. It is only then that people know that they have been heard.

When we get personal alignment with a member's inherent motivation, one achieves momentum. In effect, the member aligns him or herself with the person that they want to become in service to a shared cause concept. Personal identity gets linked to the

---

[134] Courtney O'Brien, "Trust," *The Practical Papers, Issue 3*, Context Partners, 2019, p. 41: https://static1.squarespace.com/static/5d5b379dab2d510001feb799/t/5d697e4798811e0001755 811/1567194708000/CP+Practice+Papers-+Issue+3+Trust.pdf/.

collective mission. When these internal motivations are coupled with a structure of high sociability and solidarity, dense networks become a powerful agent of social change.

The aspirational goal of an effective dense network is the combination of mission, motivation, and matter. What is missing in typical networks is that members do not have the opportunity to align their own *motivations* to a concrete mission. They may have aligned themselves to a general mission but lack the opportunity to establish personal ownership or motivational alignment in that *mission*. One needs to be more than a purpose-oriented brand. What is needed is to create an opportunity for members to develop a shared identity with the network and have the opportunity given to the network from their area of strength and motivation. They need to feel like their voice and ideas *matter*.

The key here is to segment the members in the respective networks by their aspirational roles. The aspirational roles characterize the inherent drives within people. More important than picking the right people (a top-down or imperial approach) is allowing network members to pick their motivational category (bottom-up or collaborative approach) for specific projects. Members should be invited to choose the role that best fits their skill set and personal motivation. They may have more than one and may choose differently depending on the specific project in which they choose to be involved. It is the diversity in members' perspectives and personal ownership of those perspectives that matter most. Next, we'll describe the six motivational categories needed in a dense network: curators, innovators, builders, storytellers, connectors, and sharers.

> *Curators define trends.* They can spot value and organized diverse information into useable collections. If a network were to organize a conference and select the speakers, a curator would be a valuable asset. We've all attended conferences that lacked this dimension. Oprah Winfrey's book club is a good example of this kind of curation. Of the 70 books she recommended on her show between 1996 and 2011, 59 made

it onto the *USA Today* Bestseller List.[135] Windrider Film Showcase curates short films whose independent voices reflect the human condition with compassion, creativity, and respect. This ability to curate while delivering an audience has made them an invaluable partner of Sundance Film Festival, as we'll see in the Windrider's case study later in the book.

*Innovators drive bold new ideas.* They are the visionaries. They may be accused of creating chaos as they are naturally disruptive, but they optimistically see the potential in everything. This is Mark Zuckerberg at Facebook and Elon Musk at Space X.

*Builders improve systems.* They are the engineers. In effect, they put legs on the vision. They think in scenarios. This is the role of technology executive Sheryl Sandberg at Facebook, bringing order and structure to the company and balancing the strengths of visionary Zuckerberg.

*Storytellers generate meaningful content.* Their communities rely on them to build relatable, sharable stories that connect people to bold ideas. One thinks of NPR greats Ira Glass and Krista Tippett in this regard. With the need for framing the cause concept through the engagement of imagination, it is apparent that this role is crucial for the success of a network. Storytelling cultural creatives are critical to a network's success. Too few networks have them and those that do should rely on them.

*Connectors recruit new people.* Connectors understand what everyone needs and what they can offer. They are the matchmakers connecting haves and wants. This is about more than having a large database of names and knowing lots of people; it is the ability of knowing how to put people together for maximum mutual benefit. Michael Cromartie of Faith

[135] Claire Handscombe. "All 80 of Oprah's Book Recommendations So Far," *Book Riot,* August 22, 2019: https://bookriot.com/books-recommended-by-oprah/.

Angle Forum of the Ethics and Public Policy Center had this ability, as does Bill Clinton. When connectors are also associated with weak ties, they are particularly valuable for broadening the scope of a network's influence. Barabási observes, "The truly central position in networks is reserved for those people that are simultaneously part of many large clusters... They are people who regularly come into contact with people from diverse fields and social strata."[136]

*Sharers amplify the brand message.* They are the community's high-volume communicators. They are the person at the party listening to three conversations at once. They are energized by new inputs that they feel they need to share immediately. Whereas connectors are more focused on connecting people, sharers are about broadcasting ideas and information. Talk show host Ellen DeGeneres is such a person.

*Mission, motivation, matter.* When the network mission is connected to the member's personal motivation and that motivation is rewarded in a manner that makes a person feel like they matter, one has achieved a high performing dense network.

---

[136] Barabási, p. 61.

# Social Dynamics Rule:

*The members of dense networks
must be empowered to act according
to their intrinsic motivations.*

*When people are able to align their own
motivations around a shared cause and are
empowered to use them in service to the cause,
participation in the dense network becomes aligned
to their own identity in a powerful way.*

# TACTICAL LOGISTICS
## Thinking Ecologically about Supporters and Soldiers

*"Amateurs discuss tactics; the professionals discuss logistics."*[137]
— Gen. Robert H. Barrow, USMC

There is a strong tendency to think of networks in a linear fashion, rather than as a complete ecosystem. This linear approach is the unfortunate legacy of the Enlightenment. If reality is spherical, an ecosystem, then a nonprofit and church would need to think of its donors and supporters as a part of a singular dynamic ecosystem rather than a part in a linear sequence. The key point here is that one's financial supporters, whether donors or consumers, need to be incorporated into the total life of the dense network.

Older approaches of fundraising positioned donors as means to serving an organization's ends: "We're doing good work here, please help!" A better approach to fundraising reverses the assumption. It has the organization and its mission serving as the means for the donor to pursue his or her own ends, treating the donor as a seamlessly integrated member of the dense network. Then the organization's mission becomes the vehicle for the donor to find meaning and the network a sense of community. This means, of course, that one must find donors aligned with the organization's cause concept and then empowered them to collaborate fully in the mission of the dense network as their skills and motivations dictates. Typically, donors are kept outside of the day-to-day life of the dense network rather than being integrated into it strategically. Core members of The Clapham Circle gave upwards of 80% of their wealth to the cause of abolition. [138]

---

[137] Microtodd. "Knuggets of Knowledge," *Knowledge and Skills for Leadership in the Modern Tech Industry*, August 8, 2017: https://nuggets-knowledge.com/2017/08/13/amateurs-talk-tactics-but-professionals-study-logistics/.
[138] Stephen Tomkins. *The Clapham Sect: How Wilberforce's Circle Transformed Britain* (Lion Hudson, 2010).

Funding for LGBTQ and same-sex marriage came from a few billionaire donors known as the "Four Horsemen (Pat Stryker, Tim Gill, Jared Polis, and Rutt Bridges).[139] Together they gave more than a half a billion dollars to the cause. Support was not from outside the dense network but animating from within it.

It is typical for organizational leaders to have an outward focus. For them, the aim of dense networks are to enlist an ever growing army of soldiers ready and willing for their next campaign. Few leaders simultaneously seek to enfold their supporters or customers into the larger network and its mission. Securing donors and funding become for some organizational leaders the "*dark side*" or the "*necessary evil*" that enables them to get on to the more useful and pragmatic aspects of their vision. This attitude is a mistake.

A stable dense network must have supporters as well as soldiers seamlessly incorporated into its total life. Efforts must be made to think ecologically about all aspects of the dense network. Ideas and cause concepts gain traction not because they are true or good, but because they are embedded in certain kinds of sociological contexts. Conservatives like to quote the 1948 book by conservative intellectual Richard M. Weaver, *Ideas Have Consequences*. Ideas have consequences only under certain conditions—so to do dense networks. Princeton sociologist Robert Wuthnow writes, "The likelihood of any cultural form becoming institutionalized depends especially on the conditions affecting its autonomy; its access to political, social, and economic resources; its legitimacy in relation to broader cultural patterns; and a degree of internal communication and organization."[140] Ideas only gain traction in culture when they are aligned to a particular kind of social system. We cannot get so idea-oriented about dense networks to fail to think of them as an integrated ecological system.

---

[139] Andy Kroll. "This Machine Turned Colorado Blue," *Mother Jones*, October 29, 2014.
[140] Robert Wuthnow. *Meaning and Moral Order: Explorations in Cultural Analysis* (University of California Press, 1987), p. 333.

It is the repeated lesson of warfare that one cannot allow one's tactics to get ahead of one's logistics. It happened to Napoleon in 1812 in his invasion of Russia. As their army retreated, the Russians employed scorched-earth tactics, destroying villages, towns and crops and forcing the French invaders to rely on a supply system that was incapable of feeding their large army in the field. The campaign proved to be the turning point in the Napoleonic Wars with over 500,000 French casualties. Almost the same thing happened to Adolf Hitler's Nazi Army in 1941 with Operation Barbarossa.

The lesson here for the management of dense networks is that purveyors of economic capital need to be incorporated and integrated into the core functioning of the dense network. In order to make this happen, the supporters of the effort will need to be aligned with the cause concept and then collaborated with on the basis of more than just their financial support. Put simply, the supporters of a dense network cannot be treated in a transactional manner any more than the members of the network itself. They cannot be treated as means to your ends. Rather, your cause concept must be framed as the means to their ends, their purpose, and they must be given a voice in the execution of the mission in the same manner as the other members of the dense network.

Political scientist Bryon Shafer summarizes the importance of dense networks for social impact when he observed: "No issue, not even a grand issue 'whose time has come' can triumph without the support of some organized group or groups to serve as its carrier(s) [read dense network]. An individual or a small set of individuals can argue the attractiveness of that issue. But a larger network of elite actors must press it forward."[141] Supporters and soldiers need to be incorporated together within the dense network. One must think of the dense network as an ecological system embracing all of the stakeholders. Tactical logistics is central to the sustainability

---

[141] Bryon E. Shafer. "The New Cultural Politics," *Political Science*, 1985, pp. 221-231.

of the dense network, and as we will see, so is sustaining leadership.

## Social Dynamics Rule:

*Dense networks need to include both supporters and soldiers in the network.*

*One's tactics must include one's logistics.*

# "ZONE" LEADERSHIP
## Leadership in a Dense Network

*"Success will belong to companies that are leaderless—
or, to be more precise, companies whose
leadership is so widely shared that they resemble
beehives, ant colonies, or schools of fish."[142]*
— John A. Byrne

Bio-politics is the interdisciplinary comparative study of the kinds of interactions between the life sciences and politics. In effect, it is learning from animal networks.[143] What this study has found is that network structure "provides a third alternative between top-down planning" typical of a centralized hierarchy and "the anarchy of the market."[144] Such organizations in a human context demand a certain kind of leader.

In the annals of organizational leadership, 1981 has turned out to be a pivotal year. This was the year that the science of leadership performance caught up to the Bible.

Leadership researchers found that there was a paradigm shift in the characteristics of high-performance leadership beginning in the early 1980s. What was effective prior to 1980 proved to be significantly less effective as successful leadership thereafter. There are a host of factors that led to this changing paradigm of leadership. Social, psychological, technological, and economic trends converged to simultaneously demand it. Two factors are

---

[142] John Boaz. "Symphony Orchestra Organizations in the 21st Century," *Armory: Forum of the Symphony Orchestra Institute,* October 2000, p. 66.

[143] Alexander V. Oleskin. *Biopolitics: The Political Potential of the Life Sciences* (Nova Science Publishers, 2012) and Alexander V. Oleskin. *Network Structures in Biological Systems and in Human Society* (Nova Science Publishers, 2014).

[144] L. Meulemann. *Public Management and the Metagovernance of Hierarchies, Networks and Markets* (Physica-Verlag. 2008), p. 31.

93

worth noting. In August of 1981, IBM released the first portable computer (IBM 5150). Desktop computers in contrast to mainframe computers significantly democratized information and information flow across organizations. In addition, since the 1960s, the number of women in the workforce increased substantially.[145]

Historically, high- performing leaders were animated by the power motive. What shifted was not this power motive but rather the perceived source of power. Leadership guru David Burnham writes, "In the '70's, the Institutional Leader saw the self as the source of power. In other words, 'Leadership is something I do to others.' The new data clearly indicates a change. The new InterActive Leader derives power from others: the team, group, or organization s/he leads. From this perspective, 'Leadership is something I do with others.' This change in orientation has profound implications on the beliefs and assumptions that motivate and drive a leader's behavior."[146] These changes were the conclusion of significant social science research compiled in the 1990s. They are reminiscent of the 1970s book by Robert Greenleaf, *Servant Leadership: A Journey into the Nature of Legitimate Power and Greatness.* Greenleaf writes,

> A fresh critical look is being taken at the issues of power and authority, and people are beginning to learn, however haltingly, to relate to one another in less coercive and more creatively supporting ways. A moral principle is emerging, which holds that the only authority deserving of one's allegiance is that which is freely and knowingly granted by

---

[145] "Drastic shifts in sex roles seem to be sweeping through America. From 1890 to 1985 the participation in the work force of women between the ages of twenty-five and forty-four soared from 15 to 71 percent, with the pace of change tripling after 1950. At the end of the Second World War only 10 percent of married women with children under the age of six held jobs or were seeking them. Since then mothers of preschool children have thronged the job market: by 1985 the census had classified more than half of these young mothers as participants in the work force." George Guilder. "Women in the Work Force," *The Atlantic*, September 1986:
https://www.theatlantic.com/magazine/archive/1986/09/women-in-the-work-force/304924/
[146] David Burnham, "Inside the Mind of the World-Class Leader," Burnham Rosen Group, 2002.

the led to the leader in response to, and in proportion to, the clearly evident servant stature of the leader. Those who choose to follow this principle will not casually accept the authority of existing institutions. Rather, they will freely respond only to individuals who are chosen as leaders because they are proven and trusted as servants. To the extent that this principle prevails in the future, the only truly viable institutions will be those that are predominantly servant led.[147]

Burnham's research provides empirical evidence for Christ-centered leadership that is founded upon relational (rather than positional power) and focuses on the followers' potential (rather than using people merely as instruments for production). There is now a servant leadership industry involving books, journals, think tanks, and the like.

In the Christian realm, the servant-leadership model focuses on this popular scripture reference: "Jesus called them together and said, 'You know that those who are regarded as rulers of the Gentiles lord it over them, and their high officials exercise authority over them. Not so with you. Instead, whoever wants to become great among you must be your servant, and whoever wants to be first must be slave of all. For even the Son of Man did not come to be served, but to serve, and to give his life as a ransom for many" (Mark 10:42-45, NIV). Larry Spear's book, *Insights on Leadership*, extrapolated from Greenleaf's writings ten principles: listening, empathy, healing, awareness, persuasion, conceptualization, foresight, stewardship, commitment to growth, and building community.[148]

There are two weaknesses in the servant-leadership approach. First is its intrinsic individualism. The focus on servant leadership training is usually cast as an individual task, which is seen in the

[147] Robert K. Greenleaf. *Servant leadership: A Journey into the Nature of Legitimate Power and Greatness* (Paulist Press, 2002), p. 24.
[148] Larry Spear. *Insights on Leadership: Service, Stewardship, Spirit, and Servant-leadership* (Wiley, 1998), p. 3-6.

psychological orientation of its prescriptions. The relationship of the leader to the group is not its primary emphasis. Second, it can be applied in a manner that doesn't get to the root of the problem—the source of power. Often the talk of "servant leadership" ends up being nothing more than a kinder and gentler imperial style of leadership. This makes it window dressing on the older hierarchical frame of leadership rather than a fundamental challenge to this frame as is advocated by Burnham and necessitated by dense networks. We need to flip the source of power.

In an interactive frame, the group, not the leader, is the source of power, and the leader's role is to facilitate this power and perspective across the organization and over time. Effective dense networks cannot happen without a catalytic leader and a sustaining interactive leader to balance the tensions between sociability and solidarity.

Leadership research identified three major motives in leaders: affiliation, achievement, and power. Those leaders motivated by affiliation prioritized the need for friendship and close relationships. This fosters sociability. Other leaders are motivated by achievement, which is the need to perform well at a given task. This fosters solidarity. The key to effectiveness, as we have seen, is a type of leadership that is capable of balancing these two competing motivations within the culture of an organization or dense network. This is achieved through the power motive, which is the need to be involved in influence and influencing relationships. *But the key here is the direction of the power: not from the leader to the network, but from the network to the leader.* What this looks like practically in terms of the interactive leader are four areas of competencies: 1) work focus, 2) mutuality, 3) paradox and complexity, and 4) returning authority to others. The effective network leader is clear on the cause concept, is constantly preparing and planning for the outcomes that are generated by the network. This *work focus* expresses the need for solidarity in the network. But balancing that is the willingness to see others as equals, in effect *missional peers*. This demands having a high degree of empathy and authenticity. Mutuality focus meets the demands of sociability. The next two competencies are the key to making this work as they emphasize the process of leadership. An effective network leader works for consensus decisions and is willing to *tolerate ambiguity* and messiness until the right decision emerges from the group. He or she is not inclined to force or demand a quick decisive (and often misinformed) action. This demands self-knowledge and impulse control. It also means that the organizational culture must accept flexibility. This is how an interactive leader leads change. And finally, the interactive leader thinks about who is the appropriate decision maker in every situation. More than delegation (which assumes and maintains the older power dynamic), it empowers others to take ownership and pride in making the decision.[149]

Historian Niall Ferguson demonstrates conclusively that lasting innovation and social change comes from horizontal networks. Effective dense networks require a peer-to-peer power dynamic and the open-ended ambiguity that enables innovation. The shift in the power dynamics is from hierarchy to collaboration. *But it is important to note that it is not a shift from leader to leaderless, but from imperial leadership to interactive leadership.* A dense network must be started by a catalytic leader and will be only sustained by a collaborative leader. What makes a dense network successful is actually the key to success in all kinds of organizations. They become the canary in the coal mine of effective organizational culture and leadership.

When these components of the fulcrum are brought together, the dense network can experience flow, where the sum is greater than the sum of the parts. There is something ineffable that separates great teams from the ordinary. It happens when collaboration becomes near perfect synchronicity. In sports there are many words used to describe this experience: flow, zone, and swing.

---

[149] Burnham. *Inside the Mind of the World Class Leader* (Burnham Rosen Group, 2002), p. 5.

In team sports, winning is about more than individual talent. It is about a culture of coordinated synergy that is able to be maintained under extreme stress and the changing dynamics of a particular game. This is particularly true in professional football. This is a unique team sport comprised of men with diverse talents and different physical attributes. Each has been placed on the field to accomplish a particular task in total harmony with their other teammates.

Every play is a coordinated dance that changes after every play and has to adjust in real time to the counter efforts of the opposition. Every person must personally sacrifice in a choreographed way that incorporates intrigue, deception, athleticism, brutality, and art. And at the NFL level, each of these players are jacked-up, testosterone-fueled, celebrity millionaires. With the free agency structure of player contracts, everything is financially oriented to the individual player making the most money they can, by touching the ball as many times as is possible in the average 120 plays per game. On top of this is the money and prestige associated with fantasy football that also places a premium on individual effort. Add to this the celebrity athlete orientation of sports media in particular media markets. Every aspect of the structural realities of professional football serves to undermine an emphasis on team, collaboration, and humility.

Season after season, we see teams loaded with talented players consistently underperform their potential—the 2019 Cleveland Browns are a case in point. The intangible is locker room leadership and the team culture. One suspects that Tim Tebow has been added to the Jacksonville Jaguars for his contribution to the locker room as much as for his potential on the field performance.

The New England Patriots are arguably the most hated team in the National Football League. They are also one of the most successful, valuable, and accomplished franchises in the free-agency era of professional football. The common narrative about their success is a story about their genius coach and GOAT quarterback. From our discussion on networks, we know that this is not the whole story. However valuable these men are to the team individually, their real value is their consistent contribution to the team culture known as *"The Patriot Way."* With quarterback Tom Brady now playing for the Tampa Bay Buccaneers, the coming football seasons will further elaborate on the thesis of this chapter.

Only once in the past decade can I think of a team that significantly out-cultured the Patriots. That was the 2017 Philadelphia Eagles. In the case of the Eagles, it was a combination of love and faith. *Christianity Today* reporter writes, "Despite the ubiquity of Christianity within football, in recent years the Philadelphia Eagles have stood out, especially after a viral 2016 video of five Eagles players getting baptized in the team's cold tub. The video spurred ESPN to cover the strong presence of evangelical religiosity on the team. And the following year the Eagles' reputation for conspicuous evangelical Christianity grew alongside their win totals, culminating with a Super Bowl victory over the New England Patriots."[150] This was further documented in Rob Maaddi's 2018 book, *Birds of Pray: The Story of the Philadelphia Eagles 'Faith, Brotherhood, and Super Bowl Victory.*

It is this intangible strength of culture that other teams find so difficult to replicate. Patriot players who do not adapt to this culture are quickly released. Culture trumps talent in the Patriots organization. Bill Belichick has brought a service academy culture that he learned growing up at the U.S. Naval Academy into professional football. Culture is what enables a team to stick together through difficult times and costly injuries to play above the expectation of the team's raw individual talent. It is a factor that is overlooked by sportswriters and team fans alike. The Patriot's "Do Your Job!" slogan is just one expression of the expectation of total individual sacrifice for a cause larger than

---

[150] Paul Putz. "The Philadelphia Eagles Get the 'God Squad' Treatment," *Christianity Today*, September 6, 2018:
https://www.christianitytoday.com/ct/2018/september-web-only/rob-maaddi-birds-pray-philadelphia-eagles.html/.

oneself. Flannery O'Connor is quoted as saying, "You have to push as hard as the age is pushing against you."[151] With the systemic structural individualism of professional football, it takes an almost draconian counter-culture to offset its destructive influence on a team's performance. When they succeed in countering the individualism narrative, teams achieve the ability to play in the zone. Boston journalist Eleanor Grondin summarizes, "Setting a tone of humility does not mean eliminating excellence—it encourages success by showing how everyone's talents and abilities are to be utilized, which sometimes means sacrificing one's own glory for the success of the team. In a society that applauds overachieving individuals outside of their greater contexts, especially in the sports industry, it is refreshing to watch the Patriots dominate the game while also pushing back against that standard."[152]

The Clapham Circle had the strong focus on winning, like the Patriots, as well as a strong unifying evangelical faith, like the Eagles. Together, it made them an effective dense network, an unbeatable force for constructive social change, a band of neighbors that changed the world. A dense network's cause concept must be framed so as to define reality, must balance the tension of sociability with solidarity, align the six empowering motivations of members in the network, incorporate supporters with soldiers, and then sustain this balance and synergy with interactive leadership in the midst of ongoing external changes and challenges. The momentum created in these circumstances is about more than efficient cultural change but the creation of personal meaning and collective human flourishing both inside and outside the dense network. An effective dense network is an organization experiencing flow.

---

[151] Sally Fitzgerald, editor. *The Habit of Being: The Letters of Flannery O'Connor* (Farrar, Straus, Giroux, 1979), p.229.
[152] Eleanor Grondin. "We Can All Learn from "The Patriot Way," *The Heights*, October 18, 2019:
https://www.bcheights.com/2019/10/28/we-can-all-learn-from-the-patriot-way/.

# Social Dynamics Rule:

*Dense networks require collaborative leadership for them to be sustainable over time.*

*Such leadership enables innovation and experiences flow.*

# AN EPISTEMIC COMMUNITY
## The Federalist Society

There are basically two kinds of dense networks: those based on apprenticeship relations and those based on a shared school of thought. There has been more attention given to apprenticeship relations, as historically they are the type of dense network most associated with the academy. These kinds of dense networks were the focus of University of Pennsylvania sociologist Randall Collins magnum opus *The Sociology of Philosophies: A Global Theory of Intellectual Change.* A parallel to these academic associations between a scholar and his or her graduate student are those dynamics seen in guilds among master craftsmen and apprentices. These relational networks are also common in the legal profession among Supreme Court Justices and their clerks. Justice Amy Coney Barrett stated clearly the influence of Justice Antonin Scalia had in her judicial philosophy during her nomination process. Barrett, who clerked for Scalia in 1998 and 1999, told the Senate Judiciary Committee, "More than the style of his writing, though, it was the content of Justice Scalia's reasoning that shaped me.... A judge must apply the law as written, not as the judge wishes it were."[153]

But even more influential, if also more difficult to create, are dense networks associated with particular ideological perspectives or schools of thought. They take a longer time to create, a greater concentration of capital, and an awareness among those involved that it involves more than just the best ideas. Academics have a tendency to overplay the importance of ideas in contrast to the structural context of ideas. "Ideas have consequences" only under certain conditions. And one of these conditions—ideas with consequences—is when they are directly tied to a dense network.

---

[153] Joan Biskupic, "Antonin Scalia's legacy looms over the Amy Coney Barrett Hearings," https://www.cnn.com/2020/10/12/politics/scalia-barrett-supreme-court-hearing/index.html/.

Steven Teles writes, "My reconstruction of the history of the conservative legal movement shows, however, that ideas do not develop in a vacuum. Ideas need networks through which they can be shared and nurtured, organizations to connect them to problems and to diffuse them to political actors, and patrons to provide resources for these supportive conditions."[154] Ideas must be tied to certain sociological conditions to be influential. One of the most influential contemporary examples of such a dense network is The Federalist Society. John Yoo, the Emanuel S. Heller Professor of Law at the University of California at Berkeley School of Law writes, "The Federalist Society takes no positions, files no lawsuits, lobbies no legislators, and gives no political contributions. It is a debating society—though perhaps the most important one in American constitutional history since Hamilton, Jefferson, and Madison had dinner by themselves."[155]

**History and Purpose**
The Federalist Society is a legal membership network that promotes originalist interpretations of the Constitution. Of the nine Supreme Court justices, six are current or former members of The Federalist Society (John Roberts, Samuel Alito, Clarence Thomas, Neil Gorsuch, Brett Kavanaugh, and Amy Coney Barrett).[156] The Society currently has more than 60,000 members and hosts more than 350 events a year, making it the premier network of conservative lawyers in the country. It is now the *de facto* gatekeeper for right-of-center lawyers aspiring to government jobs and federal judgeships under Republican presidents. No one now questions its sustained influence in American society. It was The Federalist Society's vice-president of its Lawyers Division Leonard Leo who vetted the Supreme Court nominees on President Trump's list. In January 2019, *The*

---

[154] Steven M. Teles. *The Rise of the Conservative Legal Movement* (Princeton University Press, 2008), p. 4.
[155] Https://www.amazon.com/Ideas-Consequences-Conservative-Counterrevolution-Development/dp/0190933747/.
[156] Https://en.wikipedia.org/wiki/Federalist_Society#Notable_members/.

*Washington Post Magazine* wrote that the Federalist Society had reached an "unprecedented peak of power and influence."[157]

This influence was birthed in 1982 by three law students: Steven Calabresi, Lee Liberman Otis, and David McIntosh. Steven Teles writes, "The Federalist Society was founded by conservative students in elite law schools to force the legal establishment to seriously consider ideas that were typically dismissed as strange or reactionary."[158] The organization was founded on three core principles: the state exists to preserve freedom, the separation of governmental powers is central to our Constitution, and it is the duty of the judiciary to say what the law is, not what it should be. Such conservative views were absent and even stigmatized within the elite legal establishment, thought of as "crazy" or "loony." The hostility and disrespect of conservative law students at elite law schools cannot be overstated. Michael Horowitz likened his situation at Harvard Law School to being an "in-the-closet" homosexual.[159] These were schools staffed by professors advancing scholarship that sought to follow the New Deal and the liberalism of the Warren Court. The Federalist Society began by making strong academic arguments for their views within the elite law schools—generating and diffusing ideas and intellectual capital into the legal community.

By the second Reagan administration, conservatives realized that it was not enough for Republican presidents to nominate conservative justices on the Supreme Court. Teles observes, "The inabilities of Nixon's four appointees to transform the Supreme Court taught conservatives that electoral success was not enough, in and of itself, to produce legal change: conservatives' failure in the Court reflected a deep imbalance between their forces at the elite level and those of their liberal counterparts…. If they were to have any chance of influencing the development of the law,

---

[157] David Montgomery. "Conquerors of the Court," *Washington Post Magazine,* January 2, 2019: https://www.washingtonpost.com/news/magazine/wp/2019/01/02/feature/conquerors-of-the-courts/.

[158] Teles, p. 266.

[159] Amanda Hollis-Brusky. "Support Structures and Constitutional Change: Teles, Southworth, and the Conservative Legal Movement," *Law & Social Inquiry,* Spring 2011, p. 521.

conservatives would have to compete directly with liberals at the level of the organizational, and not simply electoral, mobilization."[160] Put differently, if legal politics was going to change, political culture would have to change first. Drawing on the insights of sociology of knowledge they created a network that created intellectual capital, served to legitimize these ideas with legitimating symbolic capital, while also establishing a relational plausibility structure that also served as boundary maintenance.[161] That these three students could create such an enduring social influence is a testament to the network that they created and the latent power of networks themselves. Co-founder David McIntosh summarizes their accomplishments, "The Federalist Society has trained, now, two generations of lawyers who are active around the country as civic leaders. Implicit in that is the Tocquevillian notion of lawyers being important for the community and society and so that's going to be in untold ways in which notions of originalism, of limited government, and the rule of law, are being implemented in thousands of decisions at various levels of government and the community outside of government. Putting them in place means we'll have fifty years of seeing what that actually means for impact."[162]

### Epistemic Communities

It is ironic that none of the major academic books analyzing The Federalist Society focus on the power of networks. Pomona College political professor Amanda Hollis-Brusky, who is perhaps the leading liberal scholar on The Federalist Society, ponders whether it is *sui generis*, unique or one-of-a-kind.[163] And yet this is simply the formalization of the kind of legal networks that existed when the guild was smaller and more localized in certain cities like Boston, New York, Philadelphia, and Washington. This is an important question from the perspective of progressive legal scholars who anguish over how the influence of The

---

[160] Teles, p. 1, 2.
[161] Amanda Hollis-Brusky, p. 521.
[162] Amanda Hollis-Brusky. *Ideas With Consequences: The Federalist Society and the Conservative Counterrevolution* (Oxford University Press, 2015), p. 9.
[163] Ibid. 10.

Federalist Society can be countered. What we will see is that its dynamics and success follow closely the dense network rules that we have outlined here.

Professor Hollis-Brusky does make a powerful contribution however to the understanding of ideological or schools of thought dense networks in her examination of "epistemic communities" derived from the work in international relations of political scientist Peter M. Haas.[164] An epistemic community is defined as "a network of professionals with expertise in a particular policy area bound together by a shared set of normative and principled beliefs, shared causal beliefs, shared notions of validity, and a common policy enterprise, who actively work to translate these beliefs into policy."[165] The emphasis on an "epistemic community" highlights the central role of dense networks to "define reality" in a contested context. For progressive legal, postmodern friendly professors such as Amanda Hollis-Brusky, epistemic authority does not reside in the ideas—as in "originalism"—but in the affirming community. This is particularly true, she suggests, of legal/constitutional scholarship in contrast to scientific/technocratic knowledge. She thus concludes, "Claims to legal knowledge are non-refutable, always politically contested, and depend more on the authority and power of the speakers and their institutional positions than they do on the persuasiveness or objective truth of the knowledge itself." And later, "Authority cannot and does not derive simply from the objective meaning or truth of a political epistemic network's claim, but rather from the position, power, and influence of the persons articulating that claim and translating it into policy and governing rules."[166] So an effective epistemic community has four characteristics: 1) a shared vision of social and political life, 2) a shared belief as to how to realize this vision, 3) a shared interpretation of politically contested texts, and 4) a common policy project. The power of the epistemic community is not found in its ideas but in persons who

---

[164] Peter M. Haas. "Introduction: Epistemic Communities and International Policy Coordination," *International Organization* 46, no. 1 (1992): 1-35.
[165] Hollis-Brusky, *Ideas With Consequences*, p. 10.
[166] Ibid. 11, 13.

hold those ideas who possess symbolic capital. Yale Constitutional scholar and law professor Jack M. Balkin summarizes, "In law, if not in other disciplines of human thought, authority, and particularly institutional authority, counts for a lot. The more powerful and influential the people who are willing to make a legal argument, the more quickly it moves from the 'positively loony' to the 'positively thinkable,' and ultimately to something entirely consistent with 'good legal craft.'"[167]

## Scope of Influence

The success of The Federalist Society is seen in the growth of its national network, its Supreme Court appointments, its recognized symbolic capital through widespread administrative appointments, its competing legitimacy with the American Bar Association, and the starting of an alternative progressive-competitive legal network, the American Constitution Society in 2002. It has created a political epistemic network, conceptual legitimation around core conservative ideas, social plausibility among its members, a knowledgeable audience for the judiciary, and mechanisms to promote boundary maintenance among its members. In accomplishing these goals, it has created intellectual capital, fostered conditions favorable to legislative change, credentialed key players within the field, and fostering a robust conservative political culture. Collectively this has amounted to a conservative legal revolution.

## Lessons Learned

There are lessons to be learned from The Federalist Society about the nature of ideological or schools of thought networks. First is that its lasting influence is not in its direct political action but in its impact on the political culture through generating intellectual capital, legitimizing certain ideas, and then reinforcing these ideas with a relational plausibility structure. Because this is both an ideological network (promoting certain ideas) and a guild network (enabling certain professional positions) it successfully combines both network solidarity and sociability. This indirection is a key

---

[167] Teles, p. 12.

to its success. But such indirection is very hard for financial supporters to understand as they are biased toward metrics of immediate tangible results. Indirection requires long-term patience. The fruit of The Federalist Society has been thirty years in the making and as its membership lists are secret the full scope of its influence in society and law will be never known.

Second, the animating need for The Federalist Society was the felt alienation of conservative law students at elite law schools. There is recent scholarship on the value of being an outsider. Cornell historian R. Laurence Moore suggests that being an "outsider" is an alternative version of being American and is certainly the source of religious entrepreneurialism and dynamism.[168] One of the challenges facing the alternative network to The Federalist Society, the American Constitution Society is that its members are not animated by the experience of being "otherized." When Republicans are in political power the positive influence of the Society is seen in public, when Republicans are out of political power the outsider stigma only serves to increase the momentum of membership.

Third, FedSoc has three very clear founding principles and/or cause concepts. Within this narrow, but coherent framework—individual freedom, separation of powers, and original intent—there is a great deal of accepted diversity. In general, the Society limits itself to the academic and intellectual legitimacy of these ideas rather than getting involved with the implications or consequences if these ideas are true. It has rigorously kept itself academically- oriented and has strictly avoided partisan policy activism. Teles observes, "The key decision this entrepreneurial cadre made was to narrow its mission to facilitating the activism of its members and influencing the character of intellectual debate rather than directly influencing the actions of government itself." [169] Even Leo Leonard's limited role in providing

---

[168] R. Laurence Moore. *Religious Outsiders and the Making of Americans* (Oxford University Press, 1987).

[169] Teles, p. 136.

recommendations for judicial confirmation created controversy. Teles observes, "The very complications that Leo's role in judicial confirmations has created for the Society is a sign of the importance of its boundaries and the consequences of an apparent breach."[170] In this way the Society differs markedly from the snarky *Dartmouth Review*. Co-founder Calabresi states, "One thing we very much did not want to do when we started going was turn into another *Dartmouth Review*.... We wanted to be engaged in constructive dialogue with liberal institutions. The underlying premise of the Federalist Society was that if we could just get liberals to think about and talk about our ideas enough, we might persuade them that we're right."[171] The in-your-face partisanship of a Dinesh D'Souza is not the Society's style. Teles concludes, "The Society could never have produced these effects had it pursued them directly. By limiting its programming, and thereby nurturing a reputation for intellectual seriousness and distanced from short-term partisan politics, the Society has, perhaps paradoxically, been more effective in serving the political goals of its allies than a more directly partisan organization ever could have been."[172] By keeping first things, first things, it has enabled secondary things to bloom with abandon. There are those who decry the academic over the practical. There are those who decry civility over confrontation. The Federalist Society is a case study of a better way—academic civility in service to principle.

Fourth, in this academic emphasis it has always included consideration of alternative positions. It has advocated for a vigorous and thoughtful academic debate. Its events often include progressive scholars and liberal legal activists. It is anything but a cult. It is a known social-psychological axiom known as the inoculation theory that ideas are always more persuasive when they are presented honestly in the context of their alternative.[173] *Inoculation theory* is a social psychological and communication

---

[170] Teles, p. 161.
[171] Teles, p. 163.
[172] Ibid.
[173] Lynn Anderson and William J. McGuire. "Prior Reassurance of Group Consensus as a Factor in Producing Resistance to Persuasion," *Sociometry* Vol. 28, No. 1 (March 1965), pp. 44-56.

*theory* that explains how an attitude or belief, such as a worldview, can be protected against persuasion or influence in much the same way a body can be protected against disease—for example, through preexposure to weakened versions of a stronger, future threat.[174] Philosopher Nicholas Wolterstorff writes, "The best defense against attacks on the consensus (truisms) of one's community is inoculation—presenting and then refuting arguments against the elements of that consensus. Inoculation is far more effective than no defense at all, or reassuring defenses which never so much as mention objections."[175] FedSoc has always included high profile alternative viewpoints in all of their debates striving to treat legal opponents with respect and vigorous engagement. This serves to strengthen the member's beliefs in the core principles. FedSoc represents the alternative to "cancel culture" so prevalent in certain liberal academic circles today.

Fifth, it is this combination of boundary maintenance on the core principles with an acceptance of open diversity on all other matters that makes The Federalist Society work. Whereas the headquarters maintains the organization's core focus, it enthusiastically defers authority to the local chapters and welcomes diversity of opinion among its members. Local programming is selected by the local leaders.

Sixth, it is a network that has mirrored the requirements of the legal field. The Society was a direct response to the liberal legal network: the liberalism of the legal academy, advocacy law groups such as the ACLU, credentialing organizations such as the American Bar Association, and legal and public interest law. The Society's student chapters, lawyer division, and practice areas as well its national meeting in many ways parallel the liberal legal network. The Society has a clear understanding of the legal world it is seeking to influence within its most central institutions. The Society is unapologetically elitist in its orientation arguing that ideas need to be both convincing and respectable. FedSoc

---

[174] Https://en.wikipedia.org/wiki/Inoculation_theory/.
[175] Nicholas Wolterstorff. *Educating for Responsible Action* (Eerdmans Publishing Company, 1980).

recognizes that intellectual and symbolic capital are high trump cards within the legal field. Practically, the key to the success of the Federalist Society is its stable leadership and patient foundation investors. This is a play to change the political culture of America over the course of multiple generations.

As a dense network the Federalist Society has a clear intellectual lever, a felt need by its members to overcome othering, and the power of elite guild legitimacy and plausibility. The Society has successfully combined both solidarity and sociability across two generations making it a major player in American intellectual and judicial life. And in terms of attention space within the legal market, it holds a hegemonic place within the conservative movement and warrants the status of a major player within the legal field. Its direct liberal legal competitor network, the American Constitution Society, has found it difficult to compete with this momentum and hegemonic status.

Of equal interest to the Federalist Society is the Teneo Network, its sister organization, which does for conservatism more generally, what the Federalist Society is attempting to do within the legal field. The Teneo Network vision statement reads, "We believe the heroes of history are networks of well-positioned people working together toward the same goal. If you want to change the world, you need to build a group of friends with trust, influence, and shared values."[176] Clearly, ideas with consequences are those embedded in a dense network.

---

[176] Back Cover, *Teneo Community Vision Workbook,* The Teneo Network, 2019.

# THE WORLD

# ASSESSING THE TERRAIN

*"Accounting for cultural change requires having a clear sense
of the ways in which the established producers of culture are
institutionalized: of the ways in which these institutions
extract resources from the environment, of their role in
dramatizing and maintaining status relations, and of the
status groups most likely to come to their defense."*[177]
— Robert Wuthnow

Using dense networks as a way of furthering cultural change
means that the dense network needs to be targeted to a specific
world. The term *"world"* used here denotes a concrete arena of
society. It could be a defined group of people such as an alumni
group, a geographic area such as a particular neighborhood, or a
local gathering of environmental activists. Different worlds have
different characteristics and dispositions, all of which need to be
taken into consideration by the dense network that is seeking to
influence it. The concept is similar to *"field"* in sports. Rugby,
soccer, baseball, and football are played on different kinds of
fields; the structure of the physical field and the subsequent rules
of the game determine how one plays.

In sociology a *"world"* in this sense is best understood as a
*"community of discourse"* or a *"social field."* Every social field has
three general characteristics or defining features: it is a *field of force*,
a *field of action*, and a *field of battle*. It is not helpful to talk in broad
generalities about influencing culture in general or even narrower
descriptions, such as influencing Hollywood are problematic. One
needs to be clear about what aspect of culture or what aspect of

---

[177] Robert Wuthnow. *Communities of Discourse: Ideology and Social Structure in the
Reformation, the Enlightenment, and European Socialism* (Harvard University Press, 1989),
p. 18.

Hollywood one is seeking to impact. So well-meaning goals such as "influencing our city for Christ," "addressing the climate crisis," and "restoring our nation's founding principles" need greater clarity and definition if one is going to be able to shape one's efforts to have genuine impact. There need to be boundaries to one's world and concreteness to one's cause concept. It is better to say something like, "We're here to clean up this river from this specific problem in this concrete way."—a concrete defined world with a concrete defined task.

**Field of Force**
First, a social field is a field of force, meaning that it is a community of discourse that shares a common history as well as shared dispositions that are derived from this history. These dispositions, both conscious and unconscious, are called in sociology "*habitus.*" This is a largely unrecognized but immensely important concept, which we will go into in some detail both here and in a subsequent chapter. To understand a field of force requires knowing about the history of the specific community of discourse. This shared history creates the equivalent of a psychological magnetic force field within a particular social world. Progressive environmental activists will collectively share some common biases and beliefs, conscious and unconsciously held, which will be very different from, say, a roughneck working on a Texas oil drilling rig. These shared dispositions act like a magnetic force field around a particular group.

This is a useful analogy because habitus is invisible and yet it has a direct influence on the immediate surrounding environment. A particular social world is like a magnet in which the historically derived dispositions create the forces of attraction and repulsion. Habitus—these historically derived dispositions and assumptions about the nature of reality—serves as the force field of a given social world. A Hasidic Jewish New York neighborhood is going to have a very different force field or habitus from a charismatic evangelical suburban megachurch. But their force fields will be equally real, and similarly unacknowledged. This includes the conscious, but mainly unconscious, myths, stories, and legends that shape a community's understanding about the nature of what makes "the good life." Canadian philosopher Charles Taylor calls this a community's "social imaginary."[178] Habitus shapes both the community's aspirations and behavior. It is for them the taken-for-granted, common sense understanding of reality and the way one functions normally in life without even thinking about it.

Consider the common Western greeting of the handshake. It is an everyday behavior that is embedded with a specific history and culturally derived meaning. As a greeting of friendship, it is derived from the 5th century BC in Greece when warriors would extend their dominant fighting hand—the right hand—to show that they were unarmed and shake the other person's arm to demonstrate that the other person was not concealing a weapon up their sleeve. In the context of the recent COVID-19 pandemic, the common handshake became a threat and a symbol of hygienic disregard. Fist pumps and elbow touching became the replacement vogue. The simplest of social gestures are embedded with a long, and often forgotten history, and socially understood symbolic meaning.[179]

There's an amazing diversity of greeting customs from around the world. In Tibet, sticking out your tongue can be a way of welcoming people. In New Zealand, Maori greet each other by touching noses. Ethiopian men touch shoulders, and in the Democratic Republic of Congo, male friends touch foreheads. In many Asian countries, people bow to each other when meeting. And in some European countries, as well as Arab countries, hugs or kisses on both cheeks is more the norm. Habitus creates the consensus of common-sense behaviors for a particular community or social group.

Habitus creates both the "rules of the game" and the "feel for the game" in a particular social world even among something as

---

[178] Charles Taylor. *Modern Social Imaginaries* (Duke University Press, 2007). I tend to think that "social imaginary" is a more useful term than "worldview," a term which has much greater play in some communities of discourse.
[179] See https://deepenglish.com/2014/07/handshake-history-listening-fluency-116/.

mundane and ubiquitous as a handshake.[180] One can see from the simple handshake that the same behavior might very well have the opposite meaning in a different social field.[181]

Like a magnet, habitus serves as the force field of a given social world. One must come to understand the unconscious historically derived dispositions or habits of a given social world. To an extent, one must "go native" in order to appreciate these unconscious ways of doing and seeing life. The globalization and hegemony of Western modernity has tended to make people less sensitive to these real differences. One must immerse oneself in the history of a social field. Americans are notoriously bad at being sensitive to these subtle cultural differences and the power they have over society. This cultural naïveté was on display when the United States' thought that it could easily introduce Western democracy into tribal Iraq. Nation building proved to be a far more difficult undertaking because of fundamental differences of culture. Harvard political scientist Samuel Huntington countered this naïveté in a *Foreign Affairs* article, "It is my hypothesis that the fundamental sources of conflict in this new world will not be primarily ideological or primarily economic. The great divisions among humankind and the dominating source of conflict will be cultural.... The clash of civilizations will dominate global politics."[182] We must learn and come to appreciate the power of habitus as a defining feature of a given social field. It is its field of force.

## Field of Action

Second, a field is a field of action, an objectified system of social relations—a given structure of players and institutions. It is never just isolated individuals, but individuals within a given structure of institutions and interests and means of cultural production. "Far from being a simple aggregate of isolated agents," Bourdieu explains, "the cultural field consists of a set of systems of interrelated agents and institutions functionally defined by their

---

[180] Pierre Bourdieu. *Outline of a Theory of Practice* (Cambridge University Press, 1977), p. 80.
[181] Pierre Bourdieu. *Distinction* (Harvard University Press, 1984), p. 94.
[182] Samuel P. Huntington. "The Clash of Civilizations," *Foreign Affairs*, Summer 1993, p. 22.

role in the division of labor (of production, reproduction, and diffusion of cultural goods)."[183] We must map and appreciate these relational structures and latent power centers within a field.

Each field is a distinct cultural "game" with different rules and ways of playing. "There are as many practical understandings of the game, and thus interests, as there are games. Each field calls forth and gives life to a specific form of interest, a specific *illusio* as tacit recognition of the values of the stakes of the game and as practical mastery of its rules."[184] Thus the particular cultural game one plays determines the rules of the game. Habitus gives one the feel for a specific game. Historically, for-profit companies and non-profit organizations operated with decidedly different orientations. In today's world of "conscious capitalism" the habitus of these two different types of organizations is blurring. Participants at SoCap, the global impact summit, do not care whether one is for-profit or non-profit as long as one pragmatically solves the pressing social problem that is targeted.

But generally, structures and conventions of the field also determine how the game will be played. To make an impact within a given world, one must understand the underlying assumptions as well as the organizational structure of the field. Bourdieu summarizes, "To understand the social genesis of a field and to grasp what constitutes the specific necessity of the belief that supports it, of the language game, which operates in it and of the material and symbolic stakes which are engendered in it, is to account for it." Within every field there are influential gatekeepers and structured institutions that aggregate attention space and mobilize available cultural resources. Knowing the contours of the world one is seeking to influence ahead of time is essential for making a difference in it. Thorough reconnaissance or mapping the world must take place before engaging it.

---

[183] Bourdieu. "The Market for Symbolic Goods," *Poetics* 14, 1985, p. 13.
[184] Bourdieu. "Genesis and Structure of the Religious Field," *Comparative Social Research*, p. 42.

## Field of Battle

Third, a social field is a field of battle in which power, resources, and boundaries are continually contested. The field is thus not only a field of forces, a space of objective force lines—people and institutions—but also a battlefield, a structured arena in which cultural change agents struggle to (re)define the field's structure and boundaries and more importantly its definition of reality.

There is some danger in using a military metaphor here in that it tacitly celebrates a militant cultural warrior stance towards culture. This is not my intention, as I am a strong advocate for a winsome principled pluralism working for the common good.[185] But at the same time, one must not be naive nor shy about the reality of power in social life. Faith-based organizations need to be especially careful in their use of power so that it is always focused on the good of others rather than a narrow interest-group tribalism.[186] Power is an inevitable cultural reality that is not necessarily a bad thing.

The social field is a place of play and competition in which social agents and institutions—those that possess and demonstrate a certain quantity of capital sufficient to occupy the dominant positions within their respective fields—confront one another in strategies aimed at preserving or transforming the balance of forces.[187] Culture as a definition of reality is always contested terrain. At issue is whether our motivation in the use of power is for domination or service. To the degree we use tell-tale metaphors like "capturing a mountain," "winning back," "thoroughly crushing" or "taking over," we are operating from the "Constantinian impulse" of domination. Faith communities that use such language obviate their credibility of really seeking to serve the common good. Sociologist James Davison Hunter warns faith-based organizations of this tendency:

---

[185] See John Inazu. *Confident Pluralism: Surviving and Thriving through Deep Difference* (University of Chicago Press, 2018), Tim Keller and John Inazu. *Uncommon Ground: Living Faithfully in a World of Difference* (Thomas Nelson, 2020), James Davison Hunter. *To Change the World* (Oxford University Press, 2010).

[186] Hunter, *To Change the World*, p. 97.

[187] Bourdieu. "The Market for Symbolic Goods," *Poetics* 14, 1985, p. 12-13.

Rather than challenging the principalities and powers, the people of God became united with the powers; rather than proclaiming the peace, the church embraced an ethic of coercion, power and, thus, violence; rather than resisting the power of the state, the church provided divine legitimation for the state, which has invariably led to the hubris of empire, conquest, and persecution; rather than modeling a new kind of society, the church imitated the social structures of hierarchy and administration; rather than being a servant to the poor and the oppressed, the church has been complicit in wielding economic and political power over the poor and the oppressed.[188]

This is how many faith-based organizations are perceived, merely as a political power block that operates with a Nietzschean strategy of will-to-power not unlike every other political power bloc. Functional Nietzscheanism undermines one's core beliefs, particularly Christian ones. The function of dense networks ideally is to be something different from a more strategically organized political action committee. This bastardizes its constructive purpose in society.

Rather, one needs to assess the world one is trying to move. One must come to understand its unconscious historically-derived perceptions on reality and the nature of the good life or habitus; one must map the key gatekeepers and institutional structures that dominate the attention space and available cultural resources—in effect, what and who is taken seriously within the social field and realized that these differences will result in an inevitable battle for cultural power, the power to define reality. The most overlooked aspect of the terrain is the field of force or the habitus of the field. Let's examine this somewhat foreign concept more closely.

---

[188] Hunter, 153.

## Social Dynamics Rule:

*One must define a particular social world to influence because the characteristics of that social world will determine one's engagement tactics.*

*A particular social world will have a distinct field of force, field of action, and field of battle.*

# THE UNCONSCIOUS
# ASSUMPTIONS
## A Socioanalysis of the Swallowed Past

*"Men make their own history, but they do not make it*
*just as they please; they do not make it under*
*circumstances chosen by themselves, but under*
*circumstances directly encountered from the past.*
*The tradition of all the dead generations weighs*
*like a nightmare on the brain of the living."[189]*
— Karl Marx

A determining boundary of a social field is a shared habitus. To effectively analyze a social world, one is seeking to influence, one must grasp these invisible defining dispositions. They cannot be overlooked, though they are much less obvious than some of the structural features that one tends to map. If we were graphing this visually, habitus are the lines connecting the various nodes. We see the nodes, but it is these invisible lines that put the nodes into a network. Though less obvious, they remain decisive. It is what makes a desperate group of individuals into an effective dense network. Because habitus is such a strange and unfamiliar concept, we will examine it more closely using the American evangelical faith community as the case study. We could just as easily pick the boxing community in Chicago or French high society. Each will have their distinctive and determining habitus.[190] "Evangelicals" are a good foil because the reader is either sympathetic toward them or has strong negative feelings about them. They are known and don't elicit a neutral response.

---

[189] Karl Marx. *The Eighteenth Brumaire of Louis Bonaparte* (International, 1963), p. 15.
[190] Loïc Wacquant. *Body & Soul: Notebooks of an Apprentice Boxer* (Oxford University Press, 2006) and Pierre Bourdieu. *Distinction* (Routledge, 2010).

Every field has a history. Embedded in this historical memory are unconscious myths and dispositions. We discussed this earlier as a boundary marker for a given field or a "field of force." Culture has both subjective and objective features. Habitus is the subjective dimension of a given social field—its latent normative assumptions about the nature of the good life.

The habitus of a field, or its historically derived dispositions, weigh on the behavior in a field like a magnet. Without magnetic attraction everything would fly apart. This is what keeps things in their place. As William Faulkner observed, "The past is not dead; it is not even past." [191] This swallowed history provides the subterranean dispositional and normative landscape of a field, shaping its tacit rules of the road and feel for the game.

They are a major force factor in American evangelicalism. Historian George Marsden observes, "On the issues of culture and politics, generalizations about evangelicalism are particularly hazardous."[192] History, Marsden argues, "is a collection of useful myths—that is, selected truths and half-truths—that define the identity of a people, establish a model that they ought to emulate, and hence legitimate present action."[193] A part of the public confusion about evangelical behavior is the expectation that these believers act on the basis of their theological beliefs and this does not appear to be the case. Rather their actions are based on their unconscious historically-derived dispositions and biases or habitus.

As illustrated here, habitus is a collection of internalized "useful myths and selected truths." Efforts in cultural engagement with American evangelicals will necessarily need to consider their latent habitus, which will impact their efforts in society for better or worse. Originally an Aristotelian term, habitus was developed further by French social theorist Pierre Bourdieu. He develops the

---

[191] William Faulkner. *Requiem for a Nun* (Vintage, 2012).
[192] George Marsden. *Understanding Fundamentalism and Evangelicalism* (Grand Rapids: Eerdmans, 1991), p. 110.
[193] Marsden. *Evangelicalism and Modern America* (Grand Rapids: Eerdmans, 1984), p. 97.

concept as an "interior history." It is the "unconscious history," the "hearth of mental activity," the "forgotten history" that history has produced and is subsequently become second nature and is coercive on action. Bourdieu writes, "Agents merely need to let themselves follow their own social 'nature,' that is, what history has made them, to be as it were 'naturally' adjusted to the historical world they are up against, to do what they have to do, to realize the future potentially inscribed in this world where they are like fish in water." [194] The evangelical habitus has at least six characteristics that act as the water in which an evangelical fish swims. [195] There are book length monographs that develop historically each of these characteristics. Here are six characteristics of the evangelical habitus:

1. Reign: A Christian Nation (1630-1800) – majoritarianism, exceptionalism*
2. Revivalism: Faith in Man (1800-1880) – populism, pietism*
3. Resentment: Loss of Hegemony (1880-1930) – grievance and resentment*
4. Retreat: A Lifestyle Enclave (1930-1970) – purity, church, parallel institutions
5. Reassertion: Take Back (1970-1995) – power, militarism, politicization, functional Nietzscheanism*, and
6. Reassessment: Cracks in the Habitus (1995-2020) – doubt, emergent, deconstruction, "Post-Protestant"

*Emphasized by the Trump political candidacy*

These six unconscious myths of identity largely shape evangelical public behavior.

---

[194] Pierre Bourdieu. *The Logic of Practice* (Redwood City: Stanford University Press, 1990), p. 90.
[195] For a fuller discussion see David John Seel, Jr. "The Evangelical Meltdown: Modernity and the Hysteresis of Habitus," (Ph.D. diss., University of Maryland, College Park, 1992) and John Seel. *The Evangelical Forfeit: Can We Recover?* (Grand Rapids: Baker Publishing Group, 1993).

Many have pondered how American evangelicals could support the Trump presidency by 81 percent in the 2016 election. This is less of a mystery when one observes that Trump repeatedly emphasized four of these six unconscious dispositions—reign, revivalism, resentment, and reassertion— throughout his campaign. Evangelicals resonated with his exceptionalism, populism, anti-elitism, resentment, victimhood, and militant reassertion, summarized loosely in "Making America Great Again." There is in the evangelical unconscious habitus, an immediate and isomorphic identification with Trump's campaign rhetoric even while his political and personal behavior belies traditionally conservative moral sensibilities.[196]

Lifeway author Trevin Wax argues that we should adopt a two-track understanding of evangelicals: the first based on their aspirational common doctrinal beliefs and second as a sociological and political phenomenon.[197] The habitus heresy of being anti-Trump is generally more costly for evangelical leaders than any theological heresy. This faith-based movement is now perceived in the public imagination more about reinforcing its politicized habitus than serving as a theological renewal movement. This may have been the role of evangelicalism in the past, it certainly is not that in today's society. This is what many ex-evangelical or post-evangelicals have come to affirm.[198]

Like American evangelicalism, every field has a latent habitus. One cannot ignore the force this has over a field. This habitus is more determinative of a field's behavior and priorities than most insiders are willing to acknowledge. It is imperative to understand the habitus of the field in which one is seeking to exert influence. This is not always easy to determine. This means that to a certain

---

[196] When these characteristics are reified, politicized, and further disconnected from evangelical theology and practice, one gets without much difficulty persons like Jerry Falwell, Jr. Habitus has a logic.
[197] Trevin Wax. "The Ironies of the Evangelical 'Crisis,'" *The Gospel Coalition*, October 21, 2019:
https://www.thegospelcoalition.org/blogs/trevin-wax/ironies-evangelical-crisis/.
[198] Dave Tomlinson. *The Post-Evangelical* (Zondervan, 2003).

extent one must "go native" and become embedded within the hidden thought world of the field in question.

I once asked Charlie Brown of Context Partners in Portland to do a survey of millennial religious nones or religiously unaffiliated. He said it couldn't be done because the researchers were asking all the wrong questions. "You can't ask a 2D question of a 3D reality and expect to get an accurate picture," he said. For this and other reasons, much of what is said about millennials is unfair and distorted. Brown said first you have to ask millennial religious nones what questions should be asked—doing what in the social sciences is called a *collaborative ethnography*. [199] When we are talking about working within conflicting frames as is typical today, this step cannot be missed.

It is enormously difficult to change one's habitus. It is hard enough just to acknowledge them. This requires what Bourdieu calls "socioanalysis," dredging up the swallowed historical assumptions from the past in order to become more conscious of them. We need to remove the filters that distort our perceptions of reality. The goal Bourdieu writes is to allow sociology to, "unmasks self-deception, that collectively entertained and encouraged forms of lying to oneself which, in every society, is at the basis of the most sacred values." [200]

Effective leverage within a given field will require an intuitive appreciation of the tacit historically-derived assumptions that govern the field. Even when one disagrees with these assumptions, effective leverage within the field will require taking them into consideration as a social fact within a given field. To overcome them, one must first be aware of them.

---

[199] Luke Eric Lassiter. *The Chicago Guide to Collaborative Ethnography* (University of Chicago Press, 2005).
[200] Pierre Bourdieu. *In Other Words*. Stanford University Press, 1990), p. 188.

## Social Dynamics Rule:
*Social leverage will require being aware of the dominant habitus of a given field.*

*This requires learning the field's tacit historically-derived assumptions.*

# LOCATION, LOCATION, LOCATION

*"Networks of senior leaders are constituted in the same
way as are networks of ordinary people.
What differentiates the points in these networks,
however, is their access to leading institutions.
The people who populate elite networks are working for
major government bodies, large corporations,
and prestigious cultural institutions."*[201]
— Michael Lindsay

The task of cultural leverage is determined by the specific world that one is seeking to influence. To move a world, one must first understand the contours of the world one is seeking to move. It does not matter whether the "world" is small or large, local or national. The rules of social leverage discussed in this book remain the same. They operate in concentric circles of progressive influence. It does not matter whether one is called to influence a neighborhood, a city, or a nation, the rules of social change through dense networks remain the same.

But because the composition of these worlds all differs there is no one size-fits-all strategy that will be appropriate to every world. The principles remain the same, but the applications differ substantially. Eventually, the academic theorist must give way to the local practitioner. The academic may be able to describe the principles, but they rarely practice outside of their own academic discipline and university setting. One must customize one's cultural engagement tactics to address the unique historically-

---

[201] Michael Lindsay. *View from the Top* (Wiley, 2014), p. 6.

derived dispositions, interest and power structures, and latent capital portfolio of each world or field. Thus, concrete intimate knowledge of the field is a prerequisite for influence.

This is also why faith-based strategies of "outreach" are so ineffective. Periodic forays into an arena of social life will have neither the understanding, trust, nor authenticity needed for meaningful engagement. Effective dense networks demand a strategy of "in-reach": one must find ways to identify with and align with the problems one is seeking to serve. It demands an incarnational embodied strategy to be effective. The social fields are diverse. How one influences each field will differ. But the approach one takes to fields will always be the same or have the same components of analysis. In this regard, it doesn't matter if the field is small, medium, or large as the process of analysis is largely the same.

Typically books on "cultural influence" speak only about the macro national dimension. But rarely state that the principles of influence remain the same even in smaller, less influential social groupings. The scope of influence and importance of a particular field might be limited or broad, but how one addresses the field as an agent of change will be the same.

If one is a professional baseball scout assessing the potential of a pitcher, it matters little if the evaluated pitcher is pitching in the AAA or the majors. The components of one's assessment will largely remain the same: speed, control, diversity of pitches, and command of the game. Every time a pitcher faces a batter, there are only four outcomes to measure: strikeouts, walks, home runs, and balls in play. The percentage of each will need to be evaluated for every prospective pitcher being considered.

Likewise, there is diversity in the kinds of fields, but uniformity in how one approaches them. For most people, the scope of the field that they are seeking to serve, and influence will be determined by their personal calling and/or organizational cause concept. Not everyone is called or capable of playing in the major leagues or working with a national culture-shaping platform such as The Nantucket Project or Sundance Film Festival. But everyone is responsible to have the most constructive influence for others and the civic common good within the particular field dictated by one's calling and passion.

One should not neglect nor minimize the call to small people and small places. As Francis Schaeffer preached, "We must remember throughout our lives that in God's sight there are no little people and no little places. Only one thing is important to be consecrated persons in God's place for us, at each moment."[202] Don't neglect the call of the small, for it is here where humility can be demonstrated, dependence on a Higher Power maintained, and lessons for effectiveness learned.

This means that the rules of social leverage touch on every person's calling and every sphere of influence. The challenge is to be faithful at the very place in the very moment where God, real needs, present opportunity, and personal passion has placed you.

This point needs to be remembered as we turn to discuss the significance of social location. There is nothing elitist about this approach to fields. Even acknowledging the difference between center and peripheral fields—to which we will now turn—is not elitist, if our focus is on simply being faithful at the very place where you have been placed. The initial point is simply that the rules of social dynamics apply just as much in the small local arena as in the large national one. Cultural influence works in concentric circles, but it works the same manner in each circle.

While this is true, not all networks have the same potential for influence. The language normally used in discussing this within the social sciences is vertical versus horizontal and center versus peripheral. Social location is a significant structural feature in the field of action of a particular dense network.

---

[202] Francis Schaeffer, "No Little People, No Little Places," *No Little People* (Crossway Books, 1982), p. 32.

## Vertical versus Horizontal

Historian Niall Ferguson makes the distinction between networks that have a hierarchical distribution of power and those that are more vertical and egalitarian.[203] He uses the metaphor of a "*tower*" to describe established status-conserving networks and a "*town square*" to describe the innovative establishment-threatening networks. The interaction between these two types of networks—towers and town squares—is in his view a key source of historical tension. This insight is not unlike the observations made by Italian social theorist Vilfredo Pareto. Pareto's theory was largely a debate with the Marxists. While Marx's theory focused on the role of the masses, Pareto offered an elite theory of social change. He said that elites were either cunning foxes or violent lions. Foxes took risks and innovated. Lions defended the status quo. The two were constantly challenging each other. In time, the foxes would become lions. Foxes and lions were in tension over power.[204] Pareto's cyclical theory of social change is not unlike that advocated by historian Niall Ferguson in *The Square and the Tower*.

For Ferguson, "structure determines vitality." The structure of the network—the power relationships existing in the network—is as important as the content of the network. For him, the social location of a network trumps the content of the network. Ferguson continues, "We must now acknowledge that some ideas go viral because of the structural features of the network through which they spread."[205] He sees the dynamic of cultural change in the inevitable historical dialectic between town squares and towers. While I feel that his sweeping historical analysis is overly deterministic (almost Hegelian or Marxist, reifying historical processes), the character of networks, their social location, and ensuing tensions between them cannot be overlooked.

---

[203] Niall Ferguson. *The Square and the Tower: Networks and Power, from the Freemasons to Facebook* (Penguin Press, 2017).
[204] Vilfredo Pareto. *The Mind and Society* (Harcourt, Brace & Co, 1935) and *The Rise and Fall of Elites: An Application of Theoretical Sociology* (Routledge, 1991).
[205] Ferguson, p. 47.

Ferguson concludes *The Square and the Tower* by contrasting the physical architecture of today's dominant information technology companies that "eschew the vertical" (one thinks of Apple's circular headquarters) and that of the fifty-eight story United Nations headquarters in New York City that is symbolic of a vertical bureaucracy. There are structural tensions between different kinds of networks—the established vertical kind of networks and the horizontal upstart innovative democratized kind of networks. Some networks are more like towers and some are more like the town market square. There will always be tension between them.

## Center versus Peripheral

In addition to the vertical and horizontal structures of dense networks, sociologists also make a distinction between center and peripheral. Generally, this is an assessment of a network's proximity to or accessibility to large-scale centers of power. Cities, in this sense, are relatively more influential than rural communities; New York and Los Angeles more influential than Peoria or Wichita. Multinational corporations are more influential in this regard than a small business. One should be aware of the cultural location of one's network as sustained national change generally stems from center institutions and networks.

This is a particularly important consideration for faith-based organizations seeking to use dense networks to leverage cultural change. They have an inherent weakness in that they have created a parallel network of organizations that function largely outside of the mainstream. They may be large and well-funded, but they are generally disconnected from the centers of mainstream cultural production and distribution. In baseball, if one is playing in a church league, one cannot expect to be called up to the Major Leagues; DIII athletes are rarely drafted by the NFL. On a cultural scale, most faith-based leaders and organizations are only playing in the church league. On top of this, their inherent prestige and legitimacy is less respected in the public. James Davison Hunter writes, "The place that religious elites occupy in modern societies is less prominent; the role religious organizations now play in public life is less powerful."[206] Without even trying religious leaders and faith-based organizations are going to be taken less seriously in a public discussion. They are not playing on a level playing field (for which they often complain), but more importantly they are not playing on the right field. This is compounded by the fact that certain faith-based communities hold to a nascent populism that eschews and derides historically elite organizations and center locations. Many faith-based organizations lack cultural influence not only because they are playing the wrong game—that is a political game rather than a cultural game—but because they are not even in the conversations that matter because of their peripheral cultural location. And this self-inflicted marginalization doesn't even take into consideration the structural and ideological secularity that automatically delegitimizes religious elites and a religious perspective from many aspects of public life.

Ask yourself these questions: How many evangelical leaders consider it a priority to have a presence at the Milken Institute Global Conference, the Aspen Ideas Festival, The Nantucket Project, or the Sundance Film Festival? The answer is few, even if they were even aware of these events and leadership forums. These are influential national communities of discourse where ideas are shared, relationships fostered, networks established, and influence gained that are largely outside the purview of faith-based leaders. In contrast, most evangelical leaders attend conferences that are only designed to reach their own religious subculture. It is a cul-de-sac strategy.

I learned this when I first joined the John Templeton Foundation as the director of cultural influence. Templeton is a top twenty foundation in the United States with combined assets of approximately $6 billion. It funds elite organizations exploring themes at the crossroads of science and spirituality. I realized how many of my personal networks were based in the church league,

---

[206] Hunter. "Religion, Knowledge and Power in the Modern Age."

where church leaders were mostly preaching to the choir. Aspiring to have a voice in national cultural influence, I limited my time, travel, and resources to participating in networks that were no less than playing in the cultural equivalent of the AAA. I made attending the Milken Global Summit, Aspen Ideas Festival, The Nantucket Project, Sundance Film Festival, and Pop Tech a priority. There I made some key relational connections that furthered the scope of my work.

Rather than creating preachy faith films aimed at a faith-based niche audience, the faith-based community would do better to create great cinematic stories where the spiritual component is latent. This is the genius of filmmakers Terrence Malick and Krzysztof Kieslowski. Kieslowski said before his untimely death, "If film aspires to be part of culture, it should do the things great literature, art, music do—elevate the spirit, help us understand ourselves and the life around us, and give people the feeling they are not alone."[207] Great storytelling with its spiritual message latent. To the degree that the faith-based community becomes a niche market, talking only to itself, it forgoes the opportunity to have a wider voice. It becomes a self-marginalized community in terms of creating lasting cultural change. Attention to social location matters.

## Social Dynamics Rule:

*The social location of a dense network will affect the scope and significance of its influence in society.*

[207] Maria Elena de las Carrerras Kuntz. "Filming the 10 Commandments: Kieslowski as a Catholic Director," *Crisis Magazine*, November 1, 2000: https://www.crisismagazine.com/2000/filming-the-10-commandments-kieslowski-asa-catholic-director/.

# THE CAPITAL PORTFOLIO
## Determining the Resources That Matter

*"The kinds of capital, like trumps in a game of cards,
are powers which define the chances of profit in a given
field (in fact, to every field or subfield there corresponds
a particular kind of capital, which is current,
as a power or stake, in that field)."*[208]
— *Pierre Bourdieu*

Long-term viability for any effort of cultural influence through
dense networks requires diverse sources of capital. If one is playing
a game of cards, capital structures represent various suits.
Knowing what is trump or the most valued type of capital within
a particular social field is critical. Pierre Bourdieu, who has
developed this concept most fully, describes four different kinds
of capital:

1. Economic – wealth and/or access to wealth
2. Cultural – knowledge and intellectual prowess
3. Social – relational connections and ties to networks, and
4. Symbolic – recognition of high degrees of the relevant
   capital for a particular field.[209]

Hunter echoes Bourdieu's insight, "The impetus, energy, and
direction for world-making and world-changing are greatest
where various forms of cultural, social, economic, and often
political resources overlap. In short, when networks of elites in
overlapping fields and overlapping spheres of social life together
with their varied resources act in common purpose, cultures do

---

[208] Pierre Bourdieu. *Language and Symbolic Power* (Harvard University Press, 1991), p. 230.
[209] David Swartz. *Culture & Power: The Sociology of Pierre Bourdieu* (The University of Chicago Press, 1997), p. 78.

change and change profoundly."[210] This was demonstrated in the example of The Clapham Circle.

Dense networks need more than money or economic capital. As important as this is, dense networks must also have adequate sources of cultural or intellectual horsepower, social or relational connections, and symbolic or widely recognized status. For instance, a social field in Boston is going to require a higher degree of cultural and relational capital—membership at The Harvard Club and a residency in Back Bay-Beacon Hill. Hollywood prioritizes economic and symbolic capital—symbolic luxury and markers of fame are more commonly displayed. In Washington, because of the churn of elections every two to four years, who one knows and the size and depth of one's contact list is paramount. "Networking" here is a dominant and necessary activity— consequently, the priority of being invited to various social events is a measure of one's standing in the political field. Entire events are planned where this is the dominant purpose. In Philadelphia, where connections to old, established families remains significant, membership in exclusive private social clubs are valued: the First Troop Philadelphia City Cavalry, The Rabbit, The Philadelphia Club, and The Union League are well-respected clubs and civic organizations.[211] Membership to them is a public symbol of sustained social capital. Not surprisingly the Union League of Philadelphia houses the Sir John Templeton Heritage Center. Social commentator Nathaniel Burt described Philadelphia as a perfect balance between plain and fancy, reflecting its history of Quakers and Anglicans.[212] "Their tastes combined a Quaker love of plainness, modesty, and simplicity with an Anglican love of pageantry, opulence and 'good form.'"[213] These historic dispositions differ from one city to the next. Once when I was driving columnist George Will around Washington for his book tour of *Statecraft as Soulcraft*, he had me drop him off a block away

---

[210] Hunter, *To Change the World,* p. 43.
[211] G. Andrew Meschter. *The Gentlemen of Gloucester: A New Look at the First Troop Philadelphia City Cavalry* (Agamemnon Publishing, 2015).
[212] Nathaniel Burt. *The Perennial Philadelphians: The Anatomy of an American Aristocracy* (Little, Brown, 1963).
[213] Meschter, p. 265.

from the TV station lest anyone see him get out of the limousine. In those days flashy symbols of status were considered counter to the cultural gravitas he considered important as a journalist and man of letters. So while it is true that all dense networks need all four forms of capital, the field to which the dense network is oriented has its own distinctive capital portfolio mix. For maximum leverage the dense network needs to align itself with the capital structures of the field in which it is seeking influence and should have a membership that reflects its priority capital portfolio. So to have leverage within a field, one must start by mapping the social contours of the field.

To get at the field's habitus, one must have a thorough understanding of its history and how the residual myths and legends are now incorporated into the field's social imaginary, its understanding of the "good life." One cannot understand the religious dynamics of New Zealand society, for example, without appreciating the history of the Treaty of Waitangi (1840) with the Maori, the Maori renaissance in the 1970s and 1980s, and the contemporary ecology movement that overlaps with the Maori understanding of land.[214] Today it is Maori prayers that are used to open New Zealand public political events, not Christian prayers. This practice has a culturally embedded history.

The same can be said about race relations in the United States. Many deny "systemic racism" without any historical knowledge of Reconstruction, Jim Crow era, Civil Rights movement, and current patterns of incarceration. Aspects of Critical Race Theory may be overblown and the 1619 Project historically dubious, but they do point to this general often-unacknowledged point: to the degree that systemic racism persists, it is this history swallowed and now embedded in our collective unconscious. We can no longer afford to deny these unconscious aspects of

---

[214] Alistair Reese. "Why Pakeha Need to Know Who They Are," *Culture/Baptist*: https://www.academia.edu/34494707/Why_Paakehaa_need_to_know_who_they_are..pdf. See also Claire Decoteau, "Hybrid Habitus: Toward a Post-Colonial Theory of Practice," *Political Power and Social Theory*, January 2013.

institutionalized racial bias. Nonetheless, woke activists are tearing down monuments often with little appreciation of the history that they represent—as evidenced by attacks on Abraham Lincoln and Ulysses S. Grant. Likewise, until recently people living in Forrest City, Arkansas, were less aware that it was named for Confederate Lieutenant General Nathan Bedford Forrest, who after the Civil War became the first Grand Wizard of the Ku Klux Klan. We are becoming more sensitive to the enduring legacy of often forgotten history and in most cases this is helpful. The erection of Civil War monuments during Reconstruction and the Jim Crow era to reinforce the myth of the "Southern Lost Cause" must be taken into consideration in one's attitude toward Civil War monuments. Many have an historical context that do not reflect our nation's highest ideas or its citizen's better angels. So the first step in mapping the contours of a field is to learn its history, preferably the history written by both insiders as well as outsiders, by those with power and those without (history from above and below).

Second, one must ascertain the meaning behind different forms of capital within a field. In Dallas, the first question a stranger will ask is not, "What do you do?" but, "Where do you live?" In Dallas, it is identity by zip code. In Memphis, people do not ask where you went to college, but where you went to high school. High school is more closely tied to one's communal social standing. So it is not simply important to determine who quantitatively has the most economic, cultural, and social capital, the form this capital takes, but what it means within a given cultural context. And finally, one must determine who within the field has the most symbolic capital, meaning the most capital in the configuration that is most meaningful for success within the given field. If a famous person in Hollywood moved to a small southern town, his or her perceived standing in that town would be very different from back in Los Angeles. Fame is not influence—but a liability—in some settings. Rather, it matters what one is famous for. Thus, the symbolic capital is directly related to the valued capital portfolio of a given field. This symbolic capital is not only held by persons, but also by institutions and competing networks. There is a dynamism to social practice such that it varies in every specific field. Cultural sociologist Elaine Powers writes, "What one does in everyday life is dynamic and fluid, like a jazz musician's improvisation on a theme. Practice is the result of the relationship between an individual's habitus, different forms of capital, and the field of action."[215] The goal of this mapping is to be able to understand the unique "improvisation on a theme" of a given field. One must come to terms with the limits of attention space within the field. The major players within a field are always going to be few.

## Social Dynamics Rule:
*Cultural leverage requires assessing and aligning with the capital portfolio of a given field.*

*If the game is Spades, play Spades.*

---

[215] Elaine M. Power. "An Introduction to Pierre Bourdieu's Key Theoretical Concepts," *Journal for the Study of Food and Society*, Volume 3, 1999, p. 52.

# ATTENTION SPACE
## Becoming a Major Player

*"The structure of the intellectual world allows only a limited number of positions to receive much attention at any one time. There are only a small number of slots to be filled, and once they are filled up, there are overwhelming pressures against anyone else pressing through to the top ranks."*[216]
— Randall Collins

Various dense networks jockey for attention within a given world. If we ask, "Why should anyone listen to what any particular person or network says within a field?" we find that there are limits to how many people or networks will be listened to at any one time. More than just the number of network connections, there is a limit to how much attention people will defer to others within the field; there is only so much room for rival networks in the attention space. A social field functions on the basis of structural rivalries. Culture—as the power to define reality—is always contested terrain. Not all rivals will gain attention within the field. A weakness in Bourdieu's concept of field is his failure to discuss the dynamics of limited attention space. This is supplemented by the work of Randall Collins.

A field has an audience, and its attention has the last word on influence. Elite networks, few in number, and those that have the greatest access to symbolic capital tends to gain an audience's attention. University of Pennsylvania sociologist Randall Collins writes, "The most important network feature which affects the fate of its members is the stratification [or ranking] of the attention space."[217] Though there are many ways that one can

---

[216] Collins, p. 75.
[217] Collins, 39.

bring innovation to a field, and one could easily come up with a wide number of different schools of thought, the audience of the field will only pay attention to a small number, usually between three and six. "This provides a theoretical explanation why there is an upper limit that no more than about six positions are able to transmit themselves successfully to later generations."[218] Within a given field there are rarely more than six manor players. Collins summarizes, "Whatever the mode of eminence, some individuals always have more access than others to the cultural capital out of which it is produced. This does not depend on the characteristics of the individuals. The opportunity structure focuses attention on some portions of the field and leaves others in the shadows. Cultural capital is apportioned around an attention space; the more valuable cultural capital is that which can be used most successfully in the next round of competition for attention."[219] In the past twenty years, institutional evangelicalism tended to be linked with Billy Graham (Billy Graham Evangelistic Association), Chuck Colson (Prison Fellowship), and James Dobson (Focus on the Family). To the degree they had overlapping associations with these individuals, they were taken seriously within the evangelical media and philanthropic world.

At any given moment in time, there are only few major networks functioning with influence within the field. The number is limited because the audience of the field or world allows only a limited number of positions to receive much attention at any one time.[220] Tactically, one wants to be one of the big six or find ways to partner strategically with one of them. There is an advantage to being the first in the field, what in business is called the "first-mover advantage." A first mover is a service or product that gains a competitive advantage by being the first to market with a product or service. Being first, typically enables a company to establish strong brand recognition and customer loyalty before

---

[218] Alex van der Zeeuw, Laura Keesman, Don Weenink. "Sociologizing with Randall Collins: An Interview about Emotions, Violence, Attention Space, and Sociology," *European Journal of Social Theory*, June 20, 2017:
https://journals.sagepub.com/doi/full/10.1177/1368431017714909/.
[219] Collins, p. 38.
[220] Ibid., 75.

competitors enter the arena. But it is also true that being the biggest and most central organization in the field is not necessarily a guarantee for having the greatest influence or innovation.

Consider the field of contemporary space exploration. Not surprisingly, there are six major players: Virgin Galactic, Boeing, Lockheed Martin, Space X, Blue Origin, and NanoRacks.[221] Three of these companies are run by billionaires, though the company with the greatest resources of the six is Boeing. In this scenario, Boeing is the most center institution and one with the most economic and cultural capital. But it is not the most influential, a position that falls to Space X. This is not unexpected. For it is common that genuine innovation does not come from the most center network, but from those networks that reside at the periphery or edge of the center, which is exactly the social location of Space X. Hunter observes, "Innovation generally moves from elites and the institutions they lead to the general population but among elites who do not necessarily occupy the highest echelons of prestige."[222] Innovative difference makers tend to be at the periphery of the center. They need the influence of the center, but don't have to protect the status quo like those networks that are in the direct center.

A contemporary example of garnering attention space within an academic field is the rise of positive psychology within the social sciences. Today positive psychology is a major player in the field of psychology, engendering huge amounts of research capital and publicity. But it did not exist as an academic field prior to 1998. Though the term *"positive psychology"* was coined in 1954 by Abraham Maslow, it came to its own following the inaugural address of Martin Seligman as president of the American Psychological Association in 1998. Positive psychology focuses on, "the scientific study of what makes life most worth living."[223]

---

[221] Https://www.cnbc.com/2019/11/09/how-to-invest-in-space-companies-complete-guide-to-rockets-satellites-and-more.
[222] Hunter, p. 42.
[223] Christopher Peterson. "What is positive psychology, and what is it not?" *Psychology Today*, May 2008: https://www.psychologytoday.com/us/blog/the-good-life/200805/what-is-positive-psychology-and-what-is-it-not/.

Instead of focusing psychological research on dysfunction and mental illness, it focuses on human thriving and wellbeing. This is its simple core concept.

Since Seligman's address, positive psychology has grown at an explosive rate. The field has attracted hundreds of millions of dollars in research grants. Its 2019 World Congress was attended by 1,600 delegates from 70 countries. It inspires tens of thousands of research papers, volume after volume of popular books, and an army of therapists, coaches, and mentors. It is certainly not without its detractors, but such opposition is to be expected in what is now one of the most influential networks within the field of psychology, if not social science overall. It has certainly achieved the status of a "Big Six" player. One can expect strong critiques to be forthcoming.

There are numerous reasons for its success, not the least of which is the huge financial support of the John Templeton Foundation. But, put simply, Martin Seligman has effectively blended the two kinds of dense networks—master-pupil chains and school of thought. One may disagree with positive psychology strongly while at the same time be awed by the power and example of its dense network achieving significant attention space.

So the questions one must ask as one approaches a particular field or world in which to exert influence are the following: Who are the current major networks and the gatekeeping individuals within this field? If I am not among the big six players or networks, is it possible to develop a strategic partnership with one of them? A network can either go it alone within the field by picking a quarrel with another player in the field or one can find a topic someone else is already talking about and agree with it, thereby extending the argument.[224] Thus one can adopt either a strategy of subtraction or addition. *What are my capital strengths within the field as it bears on the attention space? Do I have the*

---

[224] Ibid. 38-39.

*logistical support and long-term vision to think in terms of thirty-five years, which is what qualifies a big six player?*

Having an understanding of the structural and dispositional demands of a given field and the recognition of competition within it for attention space serves as the strategic and tactical wisdom one needs to assert effective leverage in a given world. In the midst of the fog of cultural conflict, it is imperative to remember the essential task in cultural influence is to define reality.

Related to the law of small numbers of players in the attention space developed by Collins is the network science law of *"preferential attachment."* The web pages that people prefer to link are not ordinary nodes, but hubs. The better known they are, the more links point to them. This is the thinking behind website optimization. In real networks, linking is never random; rather, it is driven by popularity, translated here as symbolic capital. Notre Dame physicist Albert-Lászlo Barabási concludes, "Preferential attachment induces a rich-get-richer phenomenon that helps the more connected nodes to grab a disproportionately large number of links at the expense of the latecomers."[225] The advantage goes to those networks with relevant cultural capital, situations that heighten emotional energy, and those that are first to market. Synergy is required between the lever, the fulcrum, and the world for culture to be changed. Each aspect must be thought through and aligned with the overarching mission. Those best positioned gain more attention. Collins found in his sweeping study of world philosophy, *The Sociology of Philosophies*, over twenty-five centuries using the sociology of network analysis that, "the total number of philosophers who are significant in world history is approximately 135 to 500 persons." The main structure of intellectual life is this competition among a limited number of rival networks. "It is not individuals, whether male or female, let alone of any skin color, that produce ideas, but the flow of networks through

---

[225] Barabási, p. 88.

143

individuals."[226] If one wants to make a difference in the history of a given field or world, it will be enhanced by the creation and implementation of a dense network with recognition of the players and its heightened position in the attention space.

## Cultural Dynamics Rule:
*Cultural capital is apportioned around attention space; the more valuable cultural capital is that which can be used most successfully in the next round of competition for attention. There are rarely more than six major players in a given field.*

---

[226] Collins, p. 77.

# DEFINING REALITY
## Remembering The Main Thing

*"A dream you dream alone is only a dream.*
*A dream you dream together is reality."*[227]
— Yoko Ono

If the first responsibility of a leader is to define reality and the power of culture and the objective of dense networks is to define reality, then the concept of *"reality"* itself becomes central. What do we mean by *"reality"*? The term is contested as evidenced by Walter Truett Anderson's book, *Reality Isn't What It Used to Be: Theatrical Politics, Ready-to-Wear Religion, Global Myths, Primitive Chic, and Other Wonders of the Postmodern World.*[228] Even if we are largely in a post-postmodern world where the solipsistic skepticism of extreme postmodern assumptions has been critiqued, we are still no longer in a world where the assumptions about *"reality"* are automatically given. So, the idea of *"reality"* deserves some reflection.

First, one must acknowledge that leadership and culture comes down to a definition of reality that are ultimately metaphysical endeavors. They have a quasi-religious dimension that includes a description of ultimate authority. Some would suggest that there is no common ground to be found in discussions of ultimate reality. For them it is only a fight-until-death exercise in will-to-power. But this is not actually how the world works. The reality of society even in its most pluralistic and partisan form belies this notion. We live in a shared world with comprehensible language and common longings. However deep our differences, there is still

---

[227] David Sheff. *All We Are Saying: The Last Major Interview with John Lennon and Yoko Ono* (St. Martin's Griffin, 2000). p. 25.
[228] Walter Truett Anderson. *Reality Isn't What It Used to Be: Theatrical Politics, Ready-to-Wear Religion, Global Myths, Primitive Chic, and Other Wonders of the Postmodern World* (HarperOne, 1991).

common ground from which we can converse respectfully. We may not see everything in the same way, but we can have a reasonable adult conversation about what we see in common and our points of differences. To define reality is to say something that has a religious character. Culture, reality, and religion are overlapping concepts. Philip Rieff writes, "World creation comprises the historical task of culture: namely, to transliterate otherwise invisible sacred orders into their visible modalities—social orders."[229] This means practically that culture is inevitably a conflict over various views of ultimate reality. Peter Berger explains, "As a result of secularization religious groups are also compelled to compete with various non-religious rivals in the business of defining the world, some of them highly organized, others much more diffused institutionally."[230] Defining reality is contested and it has a metaphysical or religious character.

Second, the approach one should take in defining reality should be marked by humility and an open-ended process. One cannot start from a posture of a know-it-all. One must acknowledge the limits of human knowing even as one affirms the potential of knowing. Overly certain absolutist affirmations will in today's world persuade few people. Instead, one must join with others in a pilgrimage of discovering an accurate assessment of human nature and reality. One can know truly but never fully. Reality is always going to contain aspects of mystery and ambiguity. Reality is more complex than I will ever know, which is why I could be wrong, and why I can learn from you. It is with such a posture of humble mutual discovery that one must approach the task of defining reality.

Third, the final proof about reality is found in the living, not in the argument. This is not a theoretical exercise but an existential one. In pursuing the different approaches toward reality, the best answers are going to be found in living out those approaches

---

[229] Philip Reiff. *Sacred Order / Social Order: My Life Among the Deathworks* (University of Virginia Press, 2006), p. 2.
[230] Peter Berger. *The Sacred Canopy*, p. 137.

toward reality. It is only in this manner that one can determine whether the shoe fits. We need to have non-dogmatic confidence in reality. When someone disagrees with one's view of reality, we should encourage those who disagree to go live consistently on the basis of their alternative views for six months and then come back to report on how that worked out. When it comes to paths toward finding ultimate reality there are not many. We should be prepared to look in three directions.

This is the fourth point in defining reality. There are really only three main paths to explore: the naturalistic, pantheistic, or theistic paths.

Many appeal to science. Reality in this approach is to be found outside of oneself, but is limited to what can be seen, measured, and repeated or the general limits of the scientific method. This is a common and respected path with an established pedigree within the academy. This is the approach advocated by scientists such as Richard Dawkins in his book, *The Magic of Reality: How We Know What's Really True.* [231] The problem with this path—as many sensitive seekers have found—is that it is unable to explain aspects of reality that many people continue to view as important: morality, love, beauty, and personhood. [232] This is what Kierkegaard observed, "The scientific method becomes especially dangerous and pernicious when it encroaches on the realm of the realm of the spirit." [233] Such Enlightenment-based naturalism leaves much of reality discounted and unexplained. It is as if one looks outward, but with one's eyes closed. Even leading philosopher and astrophysicist Dartmouth's Marcelo Gleiser finds such approaches wanting. He warns, "Because much of Nature remains hidden from us, our view of the world is based on the

---

[231] Richard Dawkins. *The Magic of Reality: How We Know What's Really True* (Free Press, 2012).
[232] See James Davison Hunter and Paul Nedelisky. *Science and the Good: The Tragic Quest for the Foundations of Morality* (Yale University Press, 2018).
[233] Soren Kierkegaard. *Concluding Unscientific Postscript* (Princeton University Press, 1968), p. xv.

fraction of reality that we can measure and analyze." [234] Increasingly people are abandoning this, "world without windows" view of reality in favor of one where the cracks in the ceiling are letting in a yet unknown shaft of light—the ineffable something more.

The haunted search for "something more" provides dignity to the longing for meaning. Here is a spirituality that is largely "beyond religion." [235] Religion journalist Tara Isabella Burton observes, "From SoulCycle to contemporary occultism, from obsessive fan culture to the polyamorous and kink-based intentional communities of our sexual revolution, from wellness culture to the reactionary, atavist alt-right, today's American religious landscape is teeming with new claimants to our sense of meaning, our social place, our time, and our wallets." [236] This "spiritually fluid" path prizes personal authenticity over external authority, and intuition over institutions. This quasi-pantheistic path is the dominant and fastest growing approach toward finding what is real. In a world disenchanted by scientism and secularity, this path re-embraces the magic of life in fresh ways. One hears this haunted longing in bestselling author Elizabeth Gilbert, "I've spent my entire life in devotion to creativity, and along the way I've developed a set of beliefs about how it works—and how to work with it—that is unapologetically based upon magical thinking. And when I refer to magic here, I mean it literally. Like, in the Hogwarts sense. I am referring to the supernatural, the mystical, the inexplicable, the surreal, the divine, the transcendent, the otherworldly." [237] This inward path with its healthy living, personal flexibility, sexual freedom, and spiritual grounding has much to commend. At its best it furthers soulful living and personal enlightenment, at its worst a kind of solipsistic spiritual narcissism. It may work for the individual but is problematic for the community. The biggest danger here is that reality often becomes whatever I "*feel*" it to be,

[234] Marcelo Gleiser. *The Island of Knowledge: The Limits of Science and the Search for Meaning* (Basic Books, 2015), p. xiii.
[235] Dalai Lama. *Beyond Religion: Ethics for a Whole World* (Mariner Books, 2011).
[236] Tara Isabella Burton. *Strange Rites: New Religions for a Godless World* (Public Affairs, 2020), p. 10.
[237] Elizabeth Gilbert. *Big Magic: Creative Living Beyond Fear* (Riverhead Books, 2015), p. 34.

which is an inadequate basis for social life and those aspects of social life like justice that touch on the other.

There is finally an ancient path which, like science, places the search outside of oneself, but doesn't limit reality to the dictates of science. Here, God enters the world without being one with it. There is an enchanted invisible reality beyond the dictates of science but unlike the neopagan pantheistic path, this invisible reality is outside of oneself. The move is not down and in, but up and out. Like Wi-Fi, there is a spiritual world for which we were made and on which our human flourishing depends. French Catholic paleontologist Pierre Teilhard de Chardin is variously attributed to have said, "We are not human beings having a spiritual experience, but spiritual beings having a human experience." In a similar vein, University of South California philosopher Dallas Willard wrote that everything living is dependent upon and draws its life from an environment larger and other than itself.[238] We are made for another world and are able to draw spiritual life from that world. The enduring question is what is that larger world for which I am made and how do I access it? The ancient Celtic tradition affirmed that it could be accessed through nature and through Christian Scriptures. There are those who are rediscovering this ancient tradition as a viable path for an external objective affirmation of reality that has taken off the blinders of scientism. Of course, the obvious barrier to this path is that in a "been-there-done-that-world" Christian theism even in its most ancient forms retains the long shadow of the politicized distractions and historical hypocrisy of the church. It distracts many from Jesus.

It is not my intention to dictate or advocate for a particular path here.[239] It is only to acknowledge that the main thing of dense

---

[238] Dallas Willard. *The Divine Conspiracy: Rediscovering our Hidden Life in God* (HarperSanFranciso, 1998), p. 82. "Every kind of life, from cabbage to the water buffalo, lives from a certain world that is suited to it. It is called to that world by what it is. There alone is where its well-being lies. Cut off from its special world it languishes and eventually dies."

[239] For sake of candor and authenticity, the author follows in the ancient Celtic Christian tradition as an apprentice of Jesus. At the same time, I believe that if you can find a better way than Jesus, Jesus would be the first to tell you to take it.

networks—defining reality—forces one into a metaphysical question and an existential search for meaning. Culture is inescapably religious and so is reality. Rather than being put off by this, one has the opportunity to explore the three main paths to know what is true about reality. The tragedy is in not exploring these paths. One must existentially commit oneself to a given path of reality. One must embody or apprentice oneself to one of these three stories. Dense networks at their best provide the opportunity of making this spiritual journey together with others.

More significant than the difference of opinion about reality is indifference to the difference of opinion. The great divide is not between theists and atheists or happiness and unhappiness, but between seekers and non-seeker of reality. For those who want to make a difference in the world, issues of justice, climate change, racism, poverty, and the like all call us to think more seriously about the nature of reality. Shared participation in a dense network is an onramp for a meaningful collective existential pilgrimage. Defining reality is not the end of a political power trip, but the beginning of spiritual exploration and communal service.

## Cultural Dynamics Rule:
*The main aim of dense networks is to define reality. However, in today's world, "reality" itself is a contested concept that requires personal, even spiritual exploration.*

# VISUAL CONVERSATIONS
## The Windrider Institute and the Sundance Film Festival

*"Now, I don't know whether a film can change the
world, but I know that it starts—I know the power
of it—I know that it starts people thinking about
how to change the world."*[240]
— Jehane Noujaim

There is a contemporary dense network that is following the premises of cultural influence that outlined in this book. It is the Boise, Idaho-based Windrider Institute, founded by visionary brothers John and Ed Priddy. It was founded on the belief that stories are the storehouse of culture and that visual media is our day's principal form of storytelling. Film combines three of the classical arts: painting, music, and dramatic storytelling. The genius of Windrider has been its ability to create the experience of a digital campfire... where powerful redemptive stories are mixed with the audiences' own questions of meaning and pilgrimage. Storytelling cultural creatives are given a voice and engaged in thoughtful conversation.

For nearly twenty years, Windrider Institute has been holding a forum at the Sundance Film Festival in Park City, Utah, for students and faculty of faith-based colleges and seminaries. This has grown to include about 25 colleges and seminaries, 250 students, and 50 industry insiders. Each morning at the Festival, students discuss the importance of visual storytelling and a particular film featured at the Festival generally with the principals from the film present.

Sundance filmmakers have come to recognize that these conversations with Windrider's faith-based students are among

---

[240] Https://www.quotetab.com/quotes/by-jehane-noujaim.

the best engagement they can have with a general audience while showcasing their film at Sundance. Because this is a uniquely spiritually-oriented audience, the questions of meaning are frequently pressed to a deeper level in these conversations than in most other Sundance media events. Most of the directors and actors are not Christian believers but have come to appreciate the deeply human values reflected in these Windrider Forum engagements. It is not uncommon for a seasoned jaded Los Angeles or New York City director to open up in this setting, become especially vulnerable, even to the point of shedding tears. These experiences have become so common and so associated with Windrider that they are now called "Windrider moments."

Every film shown at the Sundance Film Festival is followed by an audience Q&A, usually with the director, producer, and a principal actor. There are times when these interactions fueled by the reflective emotion of having just seen the film turn magical— where there is a truly transcendent human connection. I first experienced this in 2008 at the screening of a small but poignant film, *Frozen River*. I thought then that if this visually-inspired human connection around stories of meaning could be captured and commodified that it would forever transform the film industry: cinematic muses gather around a digital campfire to create a human moment that points to transcendent meaning. This is what Windrider has figured out how to do: to combine the curation of powerful stories with powerful conversations about topics that further human flourishing and the common good. Windrider has become a safe place for deep conversations about the human condition, the search for meaning, in an effort to define reality.

This episodic relational magic was not the initial intent of Windrider, but it did become a lasting legacy and a known aspect of Windrider's public brand. Through the word-of-mouth of Sundance filmmakers, such as Andrew Heckler, director of *Burden* (2018), the Festival leaders became increasingly aware of Windrider. At this point, Windrider is one of the largest, single block purchasers of any group at the Sundance Film Festival, to the tune of $100,000 at each festival. Moreover, Windrider is able to attract a younger demographic that is in high demand by the Festival but who typically find the cost of the Sundance experience prohibitive. Windrider is able to offer students a Sundance experience and Windrider Forum for $250 per student, because it is housing students in the homes of the faith-based community in Park City. Windrider developed strong partnerships with the local evangelical churches as well as the Mormon and Catholic communities. On one night of the Festival, Windrider hosts a private screening for these host families and their communities. And finally, Sundance realized that Windrider, in spite of being an openly faith-based educational nonprofit, was operating consistently within the scope of the broadly humanistic values that the Sundance Institute affirmed. Sundance Institute asked if it could enter into a formal partnership with Windrider. Sundance is considered the premiere U.S. independent film festival.[241] It is where filmmakers who have something important to say showcase films. From politically fraught documentaries to explorations of transgressive sexuality to stories of redemption, these are films that embody the human drama in all of its sadness and joy, brokenness and potentiality in ways that few other mediums can match. Irene Brodsky's film, *Moonlight Sonata: Deafness in Three Movements* (2019), combines the beauty of Beethoven's music, comparing Beethoven's struggle with deafness with the existential experience of a deaf boy learning to play the piece. More than a statement about overcoming loss, it is a story that celebrates the human spirit in a manner that reveals the potential of shalom. Cy Dodson's film, *Beneath the Ink* (2018), tells the true story of Ohio tattoo artist Billy Joe White who offers to cover up racist and violent tattoos for free. It is a story that reveals the possibility of change in one Appalachian community. We see depictions of lynching turned into an American eagle and a Nazi swastika turned into a flower. Andrew Heckler's 2018 film *Burden* tells the true story of when a museum celebrating the Ku Klux Klan opens in a small South Carolina town. It is the story about Mike Burden, a

---

[241] The top five are Cannes, Venice, Berlin, Toronto, and Sundance. Sundance being the only one in the U.S.

Klansman, who is befriended by an idealistic Black preacher. *Burden* was the Audience Award winner at the Sundance Film Festival in 2018. It is a story of racial justice set in the context of human redemption and friendship.

The 250 young aspiring filmmakers and future faith-based leaders have an experience with some of the greatest films and most thoughtful filmmakers in the context of an open-handed, culturally-engaged faith. These aspiring young people learn that cultural transformative storytelling cannot be left to the Hollywood studios that continue to appeal to the lowest common denominator of adolescent audiences (sex, violence, and superheroes). What has emerged from Windrider's faithful exploration of cinematic storytelling at the Sundance Film Festival is a network of storytelling cultural creatives operating from within a faith-friendly and faithfully present perspective. Windrider hosts the Windrider Student Film Festival honoring films with themes such as redemption, resilience, social justice, equality, diversity, freedom, spirituality, dignity, purpose, and the triumph of the human spirit. These are films directed to a general Sundance audience, not a niche faith-based market. Windrider Institute is a case study in developing a network of storytelling cultural creatives who are exhibiting a commitment to human flourishing and the common good among a center institution of cultural production.

The added legitimacy of having the full support of Sundance Film Festival behind it and Sundance's need to pivot to a virtual festival in 2021 has created for Windrider the opportunity to partner with emerging distribution platforms to now deliver globally their unique point of view and leverage their powerful relational conversations. It now has a means of curating content, curating an audience, and curating conversations in a financially viable manner through the launch of Windrider Studios. This is expanding the scope of the network. For example, Windrider was supposed to attend the 2020 Q Conference in Nashville to showcase three short films to a live audience of 2,000. Instead, because of the COVID-19 pandemic, the event was done remotely, including the featured Windrider Q&A with the filmmakers and principal actors, but now to an audience of 8,000. Windrider Studios has created a packaged event that successfully captures the magic of a Windrider digital campfire moment without having to attend the Sundance Film Festival. It has commodified the magic of the Sundance Q&A. This is big. Windrider now has developed partnerships with different distribution platforms, expanding the scope of its influence exponentially.

The entertainment industry is fragmenting, putting huge burdens on the standard "tentpole" general audience films. Only a fraction of films are seen and even fewer return a profit. With the growth in digital distribution, there is a desperate need for more cinematic content. Missing in this mix is exactly what Windrider is able to provide: curated content, for a curated audience, to the end of a curated conversation. What started with an episodic human connection became a valued network and has now become a valued curator of film content and conversations through a network of partner platforms. *Period. End of Sentence,* a Windrider film, was the Winner of the 2019 Academy Award for Best Documentary Short Subject. Windrider is now positioned for industry-wide influence and leverage.

Let's highlight the successful aspects of this network. It has remained true to its grounding faith mission. It has mobilized an expanding network of storytelling cultural creatives. It has found a way to create a life transformative experience around a digital campfire by fostering human connection around imaginative engagements of meaning. It has found a way to partner with a center institution within the sphere of cultural production and further enhance the value of their partnership. And it has been able to do all this in a manner that is economically sustainable.

Faith is not a dominant theme at Sundance, and Christianity is a decidedly minority perspective. Windrider has been faithfully present over many years, quietly increasing in number, and aligned its interests with making Sundance Film Festival successful.

Windrider is in the business of defining reality through visual storytelling. But in doing so, it is also redefining the reality of faithfully present cultural engagement. They have shown that faithfulness is not feistiness. Spirituality is not fostering we/they attitudes. Rather, it is being a winsome presence that affirms the other, enters into the drama of the human condition with gentleness and tears, and creates onramps for others to share in a collaborative spiritual pilgrimage. It will take another twenty years to fully appreciate what Windrider is achieving culturally. But they are now positioned to make a significant difference through their dense network in the coming years.

# CONCLUSION

# THE DIFFERENCE IT MAKES

*"Often the biggest changes in history are the
achievements of thinly documented,
informally organized groups of people."*[242]
— Niall Ferguson

There is an African proverb that states, "If you want to go fast, *go alone. If you want to go far, go together."* Dense networks are an incarnation of *going together.* If you're serious about making a difference in society or influencing culture, then it's time to understand the power of organizations united in a compelling cause. Social science and network science affirm that the main actor on the stage of social change is not the lone individual but the dense network.

What difference does it really make to invest in a dense network?

Over the past decades, there have been numerous groups that have rallied their fundraising constituents with claims of "winning the world" or "reshaping culture" by such and such a date, usually by mass mobilization or political activism. Academically, this is nonsense. Cultural change is slow, difficult, incremental, and unpredictable. However, it does happen. There are numerous historical examples of dense networks making significant changes in society to the point of redefining reality: the rise of Christianity, the abolition of slavery, the rise of Russian communism, Jewish admission to elite universities, the Civil Rights Movement, and the LGBTQ+ equality movement. We have explored several of these examples in more depth here. Dense networks are the way things get done in society.

---

[242] Ferguson. *The Square and the Tower,* p. xix.

A mere collection of people or networks is not actually a dense network. The difference is the degree to which people have aligned themselves—and ideally their own motivations—to a shared cause. A dense network requires balancing a high degree of missional solidarity with relational sociality. A disparate collection of people must be consciously mobilized toward collective action.

These are the weaknesses of most faith-based organizations, who talk warmly of "community," but do little to mobilize its collective potential. There may be talk of individually reaching a particular city or neighborhood, but the emphasis continues to be on individual action rather than collective mobilization. Other organizations have a failure of imagination. They don't embrace with any confidence a big picture cause—the parallel to the abolition of slavery or equal rights for the LGBTQ+ community. Painting a particular school is hardly the same thing as reducing the illiteracy rates of elementary age students in a city. We tend to not think big enough. There is an emerging business movement of triple-bottom-line companies (people + planet + profit) associated with B Corps. Patagonia is a company committed to big picture ecological thinking. Patagonia's corporate goal is not to sell clothes or climbing equipment, but to use the business as a means of recruiting people for environmental activism to address the climate crisis. They invest one percent of their profits in supporting environmental groups. They are active in training environmental activists. But in spite of all their past efforts and financial investments, they felt that they were not doing enough in the light of the impending climate crisis, so they added a strategy called Patagonia Action Works. [243] Their general awareness that a network strategy was necessary is commendable. However, on closer examination their effort does not go far enough. Their focus is only on "recruitment," not on mobilization. They have used a social media app to help connect their customers with local groups to which they have provided environmental financial support, providing additional manpower for their grantees. One might think of Patagonia Action Works as a dating

---

[243] Https://www.patagonia.com/actionworks/about/.

app for environmental activists. This is a necessary first step but is not sufficient to mobilize a dense network. It is my impression that they are gathering groups around a local environmental need but are not empowering these groups once organized to be maximally effective. They are building networks, but not ones that are sufficiently dense according to the rules of network science. Recruitment is not mobilization.

Likewise, the Faith Angle Forum is a group of center-institution journalists who meet regularly to better inform their journalistic writing on matters of faith and democracy. Like the typical church-community, their focus is on better equipping themselves rather than collectively providing leadership to the crisis of journalistic legitimacy that prevails in American society. This is a squandered opportunity when the public confidence in mainstream media and journalism is collapsing. This is a network that could be meaningfully mobilized to address the public perception of "fake news," which is systemically undermining the fourth estate of democracy. The Victorian writer Thomas Carlyle called the press the "Fourth Estate of the Realm." By this he meant that it acted as a sort of watchdog of the constitution and, as such, formed a vital part of democratic government. However, with the ideological fragmentation of cable news, with the collapse of a shared national press because of social media, the reality of partisan politics, the delegitimization of journalism is more than just a professional crisis but a national one. Merely writing periodic Op-Eds on the topic, as say, David Brooks is apt to do in *The New York Times*, is not nearly adequate to the systemic changes that are necessary if this crisis of journalistic legitimacy is to be abated. This opportunity remains.

Few institutions have suffered more from the COVID-19 pandemic than colleges and universities. Most of the 4,500 colleges and universities in the United States are heavily dependent on admission tuition for their survival. These are institutions that exist with little financial elasticity. On top of this, university leadership are all aware of the coming changes in demographics that will significantly reduce the pool of potential college freshmen. "The bottom line is that many of the nation's colleges and universities will face declining or stagnant student enrollment rates beginning in about six years, a reality which will require a thoughtful, strategic approach to ensure the viability and sustainability of those institutions."[244] This coming reality is now accelerated by the pandemic and by the changing attitudes of students towards the economic value of a college degree. Most second-tier colleges and universities are facing a crisis of survival. Admissions for the Fall 2021 are down on average ten percent in total applications.[245] The late Harvard Business School Professor Clayton Christensen predicts in *Forbes* that fifty percent of colleges and universities will close or go bankrupt in the next decade.[246]

And yet, all of these institutions have organized existing networks of alumni. Few of them have been mobilized as a dense network to assist in this potential admissions crisis. Rather than integrating development, alumni relations, and admissions, these vital institutional functions remain departmentally siloed and rarely mobilized around a shared cause. Everyone knows that "word-of-mouth" advertising is the most effective. These alumni networks are wasted potential dense networks. There are some exceptions to the rule. Grove City College has a powerful alumni network. In the midst of the pandemic, over 3,000 alumni attended the carefully planned alumni weekend in the fall of 2020. To the administration's surprise, admissions numbers increased during the pandemic admissions cycle. For most colleges and universities mobilizing their latent networks in service to admissions is going to be a necessity.

---

[244] Missy Cline, "The Looming Higher Ed Enrollment Cliff," https://www.cupahr.org/issue/feature/higher-ed-enrollment-cliff/.
[245] Https://www.insidehighered.com/admissions/article/2021/02/01/full-story-admissions-isnt-just-what-youve-been-reading/.
[246] Michael Horn. "Will Half of All Colleges Really Close in the Next Decade?," *Forbes*, December 13, 2018: https://www.forbes.com/sites/michaelhorn/2018/12/13/will-half-of-all-colleges-really-close-in-the-next-decade/?sh=7a51284452e5/.

All philanthropic organizations are organized around a limited set of funding priorities, known as "donor intent." Over the years of providing grants, they have a wide number of grantees who are involved in common activities around which the foundation is deeply committed. Few foundations have sought to mobilize these grantees as a dense network. Some foundations host conferences for grantees on an annual basis, but few foundations mobilize their grantees toward a larger cause concept in spite of the grantee's indebtedness to the foundation. Participation in an ongoing dense network could easily be stipulated as a condition of their grant, thereby furthering the impact and reach of the foundation's financial investment.

Think tanks and research centers typically advocate for a defined political ideology or school of thought. The more academically-oriented organizations have typically depended on traditional mentoring relationships (faculty, graduate, and postdoctoral students) as the basis of their networks. In some of these organizations, the school of thought remains latent and ill-defined as it is not clear enough to be articulated as an organizing cause concept. In most cases, the school of thought when actually defined is not able to be articulated in a simple straightforward manner. In the academy, high marks are given to complexity and ambiguity, the academic "on the other hand..." In addition, most academic scholars are not known as catalytic charismatic leaders as academic decorum and departmental deference generally precludes such presentations of self. The counterexample of Martin Seligman and positive psychology as well as The Federalist Society proves the power of dense networks organized around a defined school of thought. Dense networks are where institutional leverage is achieved.

In American society, collaboration is rarely rewarded. We prefer the lone winner, the championed genius, the celebrity who graces the cover of *People* or *Christianity Today* magazines. The power of dense networks is a much harder story to tell and so the narrative about their power to make lasting social change is muted. It is often only in the hindsight of history that their importance

162

becomes apparent as seen in historian Niall Ferguson's book *The Square and the Tower.*

Network science has shown that not only does much of natural reality function as a dense network, but also that it does so according to strict rules. Organizational leaders who want to make a difference in the world, who want to expand their market share, who want to mobilize the loyalty of their customers, who want to leave a lasting legacy would do well to reevaluate the priority they place on establishing a dense network within their field of influence. For some, it is about more than success, it may be the difference in their long-term survival.

# DENSE NETWORKS AS
# FAITHFUL PRESENCE

*"The philosophers have only interpreted the world, in various ways. The point, however, is to change it."*[247]
— Karl Marx

*"I have argued that cultural change at its most profound level occurs through dense networks of elites operating in common purpose within institutions at the high-prestige centers of cultural production."*[248]
— James Davison Hunter

There are those who want to talk about social theory and there are others who want to use social theory to make a difference. On this, I'm with Marx. This book is for those who want to do more than merely interpret the world, but who are committed to changing it.

Social worlds, just like every other aspect of reality, have normative scientific rules. Most fundamentally is the fact that reality is essentially relational and configured as an ecology of dense networks. The notion that one can change the world by the accumulation of individual action is to deny the Trinitarian relational nature of reality. It is the group that matters more than the individual, the extended family system over the particular son or daughter.

The academic discussion of dense networks is scattered across diverse siloed academic fields, some treating the subject as a mathematical formula rather than a social dynamic. While dense

---

[247] Karl Marx. "Eleven Theses on Feuerbach," in *The German Ideology* (Prometheus Books, 1998), p. 569.
[248] Hunter. *To Change the World*, p. 274. This book is simply an explication of Hunter's thesis.

networks are surely more complicated than the picture provided here, the heuristic picture of lever, fulcrum, and world can help to organize the social rules of dense networks. This picture can help one examine one's own network and assess how one can work to make it more effective as an instrument of constructive social change. There are some additional aspects of networks that apply to computer programming and social media networks. Typically, in these discussions *"people"* are referred to as *"nodes."* This book keeps the focus on people and the social dynamics that reflect how people associate with one another.

There is a legitimate concern among social activists that the mobilizing of dense networks takes too much time; time some crises like climate change may not have. Among the case studies discussed here, it typically took 30-40 years before the dense networks were able to see measurable social change. This is not surprising in that sociologist Randall Collins indicates that the measure of a dense network's effectiveness is whether it crosses from one generation to the next. He writes, "A 33-year-period is the approximate length of an intellectual's creative work. By the end of that time, a cohort of thinkers will be virtually replaced by a new adult generation. Generational periods constitute a more or less minimal unit for structural change in an intellectual attention space."[249] This is in fact what we have seen through these historical examples.

This fact may be frustrating for some activists to the point of abandoning a dense network strategy. Here are a couple of alternative considerations.

First, there does not seem to be a sociological alternative for lasting social change. Sociologists make a distinction between *"climate"* and *"weather."* Weather is transitory and changes in a short period of time. Climate change is structural involving a much longer time frame. Dense networks are most effective on addressing matters of *"climate"* not *"weather."* However, one

---

[249] Collins, p. xix.

should also note that the case studies we explored are almost all macro-social issues. There are applications of dense networks on smaller and more localized micro-social issues in which the timeframe is greatly shortened. Moreover, most of the dense network case studies we explored happened organically without any organizational or catalytic leadership intention. When the principles of network science are consciously adopted the impact of a dense network can happen much more quickly than thirty years. The real timely aspect of dense networks is initially establishing the platform. Once it is established, accelerating the growth and impact can happen in an exponential fashion. So dense networks are not necessarily a generational strategy, even while lasting social change is typically measured in generational units. Even stopping the obviously racist quota system for Jewish admissions to elite universities took over twenty-five years.[250] Here too it was a dense network of Jewish intellectuals and academics that pushed this cause forward between 1940 and 1960. The lesson here is that real cultural change is difficult and takes time. Nonetheless, there is no value in bypassing the role of dense networks.

There are many groups of people who feel increasingly marginalized by advanced modernity. Many people feel that their social influence waning. How one responds to this fact is telling. One can deny it and carry on as before. One can whine and complain about the unfairness of it all—playing the victim. Neither of these responses are particularly helpful.

The most typical response is to align with the coercive power of the state—through presidential politics, direct legislation, or Supreme Court nominations—to bolster one's growing cultural and demographic insecurity. Both denial and reassertion in these manners are failed strategies.

When social change is needed, we have seen numerous examples of groups and organizations turning to the power of dense

---

[250] Dan Oren. *Joining the Club: Jews and Yale* (Yale University Press, 1986).

networks. How did the unorthodox beliefs of a small and disdained Jewish sect come to form the basis of the Western world's dominant religion? Baylor sociologist Rodney Stark explores this question in his book, *The Rise of Christianity*. Among his sociological findings, he found both the importance of networks in conversion, particularly networks with weak ties, among the social and cultural elites.[251] When one is socially marginal as Christians were in the first two centuries, dense networks of influential persons in urban centers located at strategic hub trade routes explain sociologically much of the growth of early Christianity. It was not only this structural factor that mattered but also the quality of their lives, their compassion during epidemics, their attitude toward women and discarded female infants, and the providence of God also contributed greatly. It should also be recognized that Paul travelled 10,000 miles personally to connect these various hubs. Yet networks played a vital role in the spread of the Christian faith among Hellenized Greeks in the early church. Many faith-based communities need this emphasis on dense networks once again.

Dense networks move one beyond individualism. It grounds one's experience in community. And when oriented toward others, it provides a source of meaning beyond oneself, perhaps even an identity. Practically, dense networks restore the horizon of meaning in one's life helping to define reality, rooting the individual in a relational context that is oriented toward others.

If corporations, nonprofits, and faith-based organizations are to regain their footing in the world for the common good, to restore their cultural influence, and genuinely make a lasting difference, it will need to align with the social dynamics of dense networks. Physicist Barabási reminds us, "By uncovering the mechanism that governs network evolution we have grasped the universality of the arsenal of tools nature uses to create the complex world around us."[252] Many organizations are failing because they are

---

[251] Rodney Stark. *The Rise of Christianity* (Princeton University Press, 1996), p. 10.

[252] Barabási, p. 107.

basing their cultural strategies on individual power instead of group power. It is now time to develop social strategies that are aligned with the universal laws of social dynamics and recapture the lessons of effective dense networks. We need to orient ourselves to inspirational cause concepts, aligned dense networks, and focused worlds. If Archimedes thought he could move the world with a lever, then we can, at least, be a constructive influence of shalom and the common good within our neighborhood, city, nation, and world. There is a better way forward. It is now time to seize the momentum of a highly connected world that our moment of history has afforded by embracing the power of dense networks. This is how we can best express faithful presence in our various spheres of influence.

# RESOURCES
## Summary of Social Dynamic Rules

### CATALYST
Dense networks require an animating visionary catalytic leader who is willing at the same time to return authority to the dense network.

### LEVER
There is no meaningful cultural dynamic without a clearly defined cause concept. One's lever or cause concept should be able to describe in a clear simple picture the outcomes of one's efforts.

One must frame or reframe the cause concept through an engagement of the imagination. One must tell a better story.

The power of culture is the power to define reality and to have that definition acted on by reality-defining storytelling cultural creatives.

### FULCRUM
Dense networks are either formed around master-apprentice relationships or a shared school of thought. Both have their strengths and weaknesses.

Dense networks must balance the inevitable tensions between sociability and solidarity.

The members of dense networks must be empowered to act according to their intrinsic motivations. When people align their own motivations around a shared cause and are empowered to use them in service to the cause, participation in the dense network becomes aligned to their own identity in a powerful way.

Dense networks need to include both supporters and soldiers in the network. One's tactics must include one's logistics.

Dense networks require collaborative leadership for them to be sustainable over time. Such leadership enables innovation and experiences flow.

## WORLD

One must define a particular social world to influence because the characteristics of that social world will determine one's engagement tactics. A particular social world will have a distinct field of force, field of action, and field of battle.

Social leverage will require being aware of the dominant habitus of a given social field. This requires learning the field's tacit historically-derived assumptions.

The social location of a dense network will affect the scope and significance of its influence on society.

Cultural leverage requires assessing and aligning with the capital portfolio of a given field. If the game is Spades, play Spades.

Cultural capital is apportioned around attention space; the more valuable cultural capital is that which can be used most successfully in the next round of competition for attention. There are rarely more than six major players in a given field.

The main aim of dense networks is to define reality. "*Reality*" is a contested concept that requires personal, even spiritual, exploration.

Dense networks at their best serve human flourishing, the common good, and faithful presence.

# Glossary

*This work introduces a number of technical terms and phrases from the academic fields of cultural sociology and network science that are not familiar to the average reader. To help readers become more familiar with these terms, here is a brief glossary.*

**Attention Space** – The amount of time and legitimacy that people give to a player within a social field. Because the attention is limited, there are rarely more than six major players within a given field.

**Capital** – The resources available in a given social field to navigate one's increase in attention space that includes but is not limited to economic, social, cultural, and symbolic capital.

**Cause concept** – What you seek to produce or the end purpose of one's efforts, also *telos*.

**Creative class** – Those people in society who are in the business of symbolic creation and dissemination of ideas, myths, and stories that define reality for other people (academics, advertisers, media, and entertainment). Often viewed as responsible for economic expansion and innovation within a geographic area.

**Culture** – The invisible social norms that combine what is accepted as the subjective taken-for-granted reality or common sense with what is the objective officially articulated reality by reality-defining institutions. Culture involves both the subjective and objective dimensions.

**Dense Network** – A dense network is a formal relationally- or ideologically-oriented diverse group of friends, colleagues, or acquaintances that share a common commitment to make a difference in the world in a particular arena of social life.

**Epistemic Community** – a network of professionals with expertise in a particular policy area bound together by a shared set of normative and principled beliefs, shared causal beliefs, shared notions of validity, and a common policy enterprise, who actively work to translate these beliefs into policy.

**Field of Action** – The given objective structure of players and institutions within a given social field or community of discourse, basically the objective culture of a given field.

**Field of Battle** – The arena wherein a social field or community of discourse competes with others over a definition of reality.

**Field of Force** – A social field or community of discourse that shares a common habitus or subjective priorities to patterns of meaning, basically the subjective culture of a given field.

**Frame** – The underlying assumptions one makes about the nature of reality, also lens or paradigm. Tends to be less cognitive or formal than worldview.

**Fulcrum** – The active members of a dense network committed to a shared cause concept. It is more than a group or community because of this externally-oriented shared commitment.

**Habitus** – Historically-derived dispositions of thought and action that frame one's view of common sense and the good life.

**Individualism** – A social theory reinforced by the Enlightenment that favors freedom of action for individuals over collective or state control. It assumes that social reality starts from the individual not the group. Within a political context is suspicious of all forms of collective action.

**Law of 150** – The cognitive limit to the number of individuals with whom any one person can maintain stable relationships, developed by corporate anthropologist Robin Dunbar.

**Lever** – A shared cause concept that reflects the telos of an individual's or organization's mission or what it seeks to accomplish in a particular arena of social life.

**Metaphor** – The way we use language to structure our experience of reality, the language pictures that reveal our frame.

**Reality-defining Institutions** – The national institutions engaged in the production and distribution of the symbolic meanings of a given society, typically including the presidency, the media, publishing houses, schools, universities, advertising agencies, and entertainment.

**Sociability** – The degree of social or relational attachment between persons or groups.

**Social Field** – A defined arena of social life that shares a common habitus, is structured by players with a given capital portfolio, who are in competition with others over a definition of reality, also social world. A dense network is not a social field but is an agent of influence or player within a given social field.

**Socioanalysis** – A concept developed by Pierre Bourdieu that applied aspects of Freudian psychoanalysis to one's social location, thereby enabling one to gain some cognitive distance and self-reflection from one's own embedded habitus which in turn increases one's agency. It is a means of developing increased self-awareness over the causes of one's behavior.

**Solidarity** – The degree of missional attachment between persons or groups.

**Story** – As used culturally, the narrative manner in which we articulate our social imaginary, or the way ordinary people imagine their social surroundings.

**Weak ties** – A concept in network science developed by Stanford sociology professor Mark Granovetter in 1973. In social networks, you have different links—or ties—to other people. Strong ties are characterized as deep affinity; for example family, friends or colleagues. Weak ties, in contrast, might be acquaintances, or a stranger with a common cultural background. The point is that the strength of these ties can substantially affect interactions, outcomes and well-being. Weak ties matter, because they bridge to new networks thereby expanding the scope of the social network. Weak ties are scientifically proven to be better in helping one get a new job.

**World** – A specific embodied, geographically located arena of social life. It can be large or small, national or local, central or peripheral, but it contains a distinctive and bounded field of force and action.

# ACKNOWLEDGEMENTS

All books are the summary of lessons learned from life and from those who have influenced one's thinking. My passion in life has been learning how to make a difference. My first consideration was that this was through the history of ideas. This was adjusted after an exposure to the work of Peter Berger and the sociology of knowledge. It was over lunch with Princeton sociologist Robert Wuthnow that I was introduced to the French structuralist Pierre Bourdieu, on whom I wrote my dissertation. But all of this theoretical and academic training was tempered by working with a number of nonprofit and for-profit organizations who also shared my aspiration to make a difference in society, in particular the Williamsburg Charter Foundation and The Trinity Forum. When working for the John Templeton Foundation as the director of cultural engagement, the question became one of strategic investment. How do we invest scarce resources so as to create lasting and meaningful social change?

It has been an axiom of mine for years that the main actor on the stage of cultural change is the dense network and not the heroic or genius individual. Working on this book has given me the opportunity to explore more fully the truth of this axiom. Among those who have influenced my thinking in the book are James Davison Hunter, Charlie Brown, Mark Rodgers, John Priddy, Ron Frey, Evan Baehr, Dwight Gibson, and J.R. Kerr. I am also grateful for Karin Silver and Samantha Trathen, my editors, who take the ideas as seriously as the words on the page. And finally, I am grateful and deeply indebted to my wife, Kathryn, for enduring the solitary life of a writer. It is to her that this book is dedicated.

# ABOUT THE AUTHOR

John Seel is a social impact consultant and cultural analyst. He is the principal at John Seel Consulting LLC where he works with organizations and projects on strategies for organizational impact and fundraising. He has a particular interest in religious nones and those disaffected by the traditional church. He was a research fellow at the Institute for Advanced Studies in Culture at the University of Virginia and is the former director of cultural engagement at the John Templeton Foundation.

Seel is a nonprofit entrepreneur, having started or been involved in starting The Williamsburg Charter, The Trinity Forum, Institute for Advanced Studies in Culture at the University of Virginia, the Society for Classical Learning, the Council on Educational Standards and Accountability (CESA), and The Cambridge School of Dallas.

Seel is the son of Presbyterian medical missionaries in South Korea, where he grew up for seventeen years. He has a B.A. in history, business administration, and philosophy from Austin College, an M.Div. from Covenant Theological Seminary, and a doctorate in American Studies from the University of Maryland (College Park). Seel has served as an adjunct faculty member at Gordon-Conwell Theological Seminary, Covenant Theological Seminary, and Palmer Theological Seminary. He is the author of *The New Copernicans: Millennials and the Survival of the Church* (Thomas Nelson). He blogs regularly at www.ncconversations.com. He and his wife, Kathryn, live on an historic 250-year-old farm outside of Chestnut Hill, Pennsylvania, with their four-legged child, Malibu. He has three grown children and four grandchildren.

Made in the USA
Las Vegas, NV
04 December 2022

61109446R00105